Elizabeth Longford

THE AUTHORISED BIOGRAPHY

Elizabeth Longford

THE AUTHORISED BIOGRAPHY

FRANCES MAKOWER

Hodder & Stoughton
LONDON SYDNEY AUCKLAND

British Library Cataloguing in Publication Data
A record for this book is available from the British Library

ISBN 0 340 69472 6

Typeset by Avon Dataset Ltd, Bidford-on-Avon, Warks

Printed and bound in Great Britain by
Mackays of Chatham PLC, Chatham, Kent

Hodder and Stoughton
A division of Hodder Headline PLC
338 Euston Road
London NW1 3BH

To Teresa de Bertodano
and Kay Killoran RSCJ

Contents

Acknowledgments

I am happy to have this opportunity to thank the many people who have contributed to this book. My sources have been numerous, varied and fascinating. Elizabeth Longford is so well loved that everyone wanted to talk about her, transforming what might have been a taxing task into a delightful exercise. Above all I am grateful to Elizabeth. She was endlessly co-operative and made all her letters, personal diaries, collection of press cuttings and record books of the children's progress available. Her memoir *The Pebbled Shore* was a further invaluable source. Her story has been enlarged upon by her husband, Frank, and by her children, friends and colleagues, to whom I am also indebted. I would also like to thank Sophie Baker, a close friend of the Longfords, for kindly accepting responsibility for assembling and completing the photographs.

I owe a particular debt to Captain Alastair Ingham Clark, Oliver Makower, the Rev. Patrick Purnell, Katharine Spink, Jean Symes, Jean Thow and Sister Prue Wilson for their critical comments on the manuscript. I am further indebted to Martin de Bertodano and Sylvia Makower for the research they undertook on my behalf; Martin also kindly supplied many of the footnotes. My debt to my literary director, Teresa de Bertodano, increases with every book I write; without her positive criticism and sensitive support this project would never have been undertaken, much less completed. I would also like to thank Hannah Grey who has provided constant and instant technical computer back-up, Carolyn Armitage and Judith Longman of Hodder and Stoughton for their editing skills, and my community; they gave me space while maintaining interest and support.

Many people answered my queries, lent me material and made suggestions. I am most grateful to Charles Anson, Val Arnold Foster, The Hon. David Astor, Peggy Attlee, Peggy Aldridge, Commander Richard Aylard, RN, Georgina Battiscombe, Lady de Bellaigue, Sir Isaiah Berlin, Caspar Billington, Lady Rachel Billington, Stephen Bird, Michael Bloch, the Countess Dominique de Borchgrave, Gwen Brown, Mary Rose Brunner, Elizabeth Butler, Lola Cameron, Edmund Carr-Saunders, Lord and Lady Charteris, Eliza Chisholm, Lady Mary Clive, Julia Courtenay, John Curtis, Elma Dangerfield, Michael Davie, Charles Davies, Tessa de Bertodano, Mr and Mrs Kevin Deatker, Lord Donaldson, Ruth East, Lottie Elson, Lady Fawcett, Sir Robert Fellowes, Agnes Fenner, Mr and Mrs Chris Fitzsimon, Phyllis Foreman, Flora Fraser, Carol Fryer, William Gammell, Anne Glennerster, Ellen Grinter, Val Grove, Lord Hailsham, Anna Harman, Nicola Harman, Ruth Harris, Lord and Lady Healey, Sir Nicholas and Lady Henderson, Janet Higbee, Michael Hope, Prue Ingham Clark, Lord Jenkins of Hillhead, Mr and Mrs Paul Johnson, Gwen Jones, Arthur Kazantzis, Judith Kazantzis, Miranda Kazantzis, Lady Pansy Lamb, Angela Lambert, Andrew Makower, Peter Makower, Dr and Mrs Andrew McLachlan, Kitty McLachlan, Flora Maxwell Stuart, Lady Mitchison, Mr and Mrs Charles Monck, Ferdinand Mount, Lord Napier and Ettrick, Nigel Nicolson, Mr and Mrs Edward Nugee, Major Richard Nugee, Claire Nutt, Connie O'Regan, Linda Osband, The Hon. Kevin and Clare Pakenham, The Hon. Michael Pakenham, The Hon. Paddy Pakenham, The Hon. Thomas and Valerie Pakenham, Kate Pakenham, Ben, Dominic and Hermione Pakenham, Pamela Parsonson, Christine Penny, Henrietta Phipps, Harold

Pinter CBE and Antonia Pinter, Lady Violet Powell, Stanley Roberts, Mrs R. Sawyer, Jon Snow, Peter Stanford, Roberta Staples, Sir Roy Strong, Anita Syvret, John Taylor, Rosemary Toussaint-Giraud, E. M. Tucker, David Uttley, Angeli Vaid, Graham Watson, Lord Weidenfeld, Barbara Weston, Lucy Willis, Andrew Wilson and Philip Ziegler.

Growing Up in a Puritanical Household

In September 1905 Nathaniel (Nat) Harman, an up-and-coming ophthalmic surgeon, brought his new bride, Katherine Chamberlain, to live at 108 Harley Street, London. Nat took a double first at Cambridge, but narrowly missed a fellowship in anatomy at St John's College. He had therefore turned to teaching and had spent the six years before he met Katherine teaching in London hospitals and treating his own patients in rooms hired for the purpose. Now, at thirty-five, he had become sufficiently successful to buy a house and put up his brass plate in the street renowned for its doctors.

Katherine Chamberlain was also a doctor; she had trained from 1893 to 1899 at the Royal Free Hospital, in north London, which then included the Women's Medical School for London University.[1] Katherine too had qualified as a surgeon and had worked in the casualty department of the Royal Free. Her private practice was to be less successful than Nat's; the only fee she ever received was £3, for the extraction of a wisdom tooth. Katherine worked for a time at the Belgrave Hospital for Children in south London. It was there in 1904 that she had called in Nat Harman to examine the eyes of a sick baby. Nat was instantly attracted to the young surgeon.

When Katherine Chamberlain registered there were only 378 women doctors in England and Wales. The general prejudice against women doctors was not shared by Katherine's family. Arthur Chamberlain, her father, had named one of his horses Lady Doctor in her honour. Her mother, Louisa Chamberlain, had developed rheumatoid arthritis in 1890 and had chosen one of the newly qualified women practitioners to supervise her own medical care. This was an unusual step at the time, which reflected a genuine trust in the competence of women doctors. Louisa died two years later, before Katherine had completed her training.

Katherine belonged to the famous Birmingham family who had made their money in ironworks and their mark as radicals in local government. She was close to her uncle Joseph Chamberlain, former Secretary of State for the Colonies under the Salisbury Conservative government, who had shown her much kindness around the time of her mother's death.[2] Joe and his third wife, Mary, had arranged a London season for Katherine in 1891 when she was eighteen. In the 1890s, while she was studying at the Royal Free Hospital, she had a standing invitation to Sunday lunch at the Chamberlains' house in west London.

The Harman family into which Katherine was marrying had originated in Sussex where they were yeomen farmers. Early in the nineteenth century they had moved to London where they had established themselves as merchants; none of the Harmans had had a particular interest in politics. When Nat's father, Walter Harman, was eight years old, his mother had died, whereupon he and all his younger brothers and sisters had been handed over to the care of their old family nurse. She was a Strict Baptist and, taking all the children away from the Anglican Church, into which they had been baptised, had brought them up in her own faith.

When Nat met Katherine in 1904 his future looked promising. Having failed to secure the desired fellowship at his Cambridge college, he had volunteered to serve for a year as a civilian consultant in the Boer War. When he returned to London he began to experiment in the making of instruments for cataract operations; these were successful and he was making a name for himself in medical circles. Katherine was much attracted to Nat, but although they had medicine in common they were divided by religion. The Harmans were Strict Baptists; the Chamberlains, Unitarians.[3]

The courtship proceeded swiftly following the first meeting of the young doctors at the Belgrave Hospital. Nat proposed to Katherine in 1905, but although she undoubtedly wanted to marry him she would not agree to do so unless Nat abandoned his deeply held belief in the Divinity of Christ and became a member of the Unitarian Church. For Nat this caused such torment that he came near to calling off the engagement; he suffered a severe mental breakdown. The anguish of his struggle is portrayed in the letters he sent to Katherine in the year before they were married and he was to be affected for the rest of his life by his hard-won decision to become a Unitarian.

Finally Nat Harman married Katherine Chamberlain in the Old Meeting House in Birmingham on 4th September 1905. Nearly half a century later, their eldest child, Elizabeth, reading the letters her father had sent to her mother during the year of their engagement, at last began to understand why her own upbringing had been so strict.[4] 'Having renounced his own father's faith for the sake of the woman he loved, [Nat] was doubly resolved to preserve his father's "works" when he himself became a father' (*The Pebbled Shore*, p. 28). This, she believed, explained his rigid insistence on the Victorian standards of obedience, sobriety and discipline that Nat himself had experienced at the hands of his own father.

Elizabeth, the first of their five children, was born in Harley Street on 30th August 1906. John, the eldest son, was born in 1907, Kitty in 1909, Roger in 1912 and Michael in 1914. All the children were born at home and although their father was in the house, he did not attend their births. Elizabeth and her mother were cared for by the monthly nurse for the first four weeks, then the baby became the charge of the family nurse, who in due course had the assistance of a nursery maid. Elizabeth and later her younger brothers and sister lived in the nursery quarters at the top of their three-storeyed Harley Street house. Three floors below, the cook reigned in the basement with a housemaid and parlourmaid, who shared the domestic chores between them. A household staff of five was about average for a comfortably-off professional middle-class family during the early years of the twentieth century.

Nevertheless, Elizabeth's memories of her early years are not of luxury or even of comfort. There was no lift in the house and no bedside lamps, reading in bed being considered decadent. The cold nursery bedroom under the roof was unheated; this the two sisters shared until Elizabeth left home to be married at the age of twenty-five. During the winter the whole house was intensely cold, for the single electric fire was in her father's consulting room. The one radiator in the hall was of little use on account of the icy blasts admitted as the front door was opened and shut for the patients. Elizabeth and Kitty were deeply concerned about the effect of the cold on their adored mother and one Christmas they presented her with a pair of fleece-lined bloomers.

Nat Harman exacerbated the austerity of 108 Harley Street by insisting on very plain fare for the children. Matters were not improved by the open-sided lift, which Nat had constructed himself and installed on the outside of the house. This hoisted food from the basement kitchen to the nursery quarters on the top floor, ensuring that nursery meals invariably arrived cold. Hot Sunday lunch was consequently regarded as a great treat. This was the only meal at which Elizabeth and her brothers and sister joined Nat and Katherine in the dining room, reserved as the patients' waiting room during the week. On Sundays a joint of beef was served, followed by apple pie. Elizabeth, dressed in a white starched frilly apron over her Sunday frock, would beg for a second helping, only to be sternly refused by her father.

She was a nervous child subject to sleep-walking and night-mares and she tried unsuccessfully to persuade her father to leave a light burning on the landing during the night. Then the clearly audible sound of the wolves howling in nearby Regents Park Zoo induced nightmares, which drove her down the dark staircase in search of her mother on the floor below. Nat was furious when Elizabeth burst into her parents' bedroom. In daylight, however, visits to the zoo were a regular and enjoyable Sunday occupation. Her favourite haunt was the reptile house where she was unafraid of the python that was once wound around her neck – but the wolves always terrified her.

Nat's short temper was frequently aroused by Elizabeth and the others. A stickler for quiet in the house, especially during working hours, he expected the children to go up to their nursery in silence when they returned from the afternoon outing to the botanical gardens in Regents Park. These gardens featured prominently in Elizabeth's early years. There, in the summer of 1913, she first caught sight of Barbara Cartland, then aged thirteen. Seven-year-old Elizabeth was entranced. The glamorous thirteen-year-old was wearing a pink frock covered in rose-buds and a large pink hat from which a mass of golden curls escaped. Returning to Harley Street after such an encounter, Elizabeth could never remember to keep quiet on the stairs. Time after time Mr Harman would fling open his consulting room door to roar at the noisy children.

In 1909 Nurse Robins came to work at Harley Street when Elizabeth was three and John two, and shortly before the birth of Kitty. On her arrival the two older children rifled through Nurse Robins's trunk, liberally sprinkling her possessions with her talcum powder; it is perhaps hardly surprising that she came to show a preference for Kitty, Roger and Michael, each of whom she was able to look after from babyhood. Nurse Robins was not always in control of her temper, which could be roused by bossy, argumentative Elizabeth. On one occasion she attempted to settle an argument by hitting Elizabeth over the head with a saucepan and then bribing her not to tell her mother by applying a scent sachet to the bump. Elizabeth realised that Nurse Robins liked the younger children better than herself, but also believed that her mother preferred Kitty. Despite his relentless teasing she found comfort in John, although on one occasion John organised the brothers into 'kidnapping' Elizabeth's dolls and 'hanging' them.

Nurse Robins had a highly charged imagination. On their daily walks she would point out to the children a pillar-box in which she said that the suffragettes had posted dynamite. On another occasion she insisted that Queen Alexandra's face was made of enamel and would crack if she smiled. Sometimes she arranged the toys half in and half out of the cupboard, so that when Elizabeth and John returned from the park, she could tell them that the dolls had played too long and had been caught before they could get back into the cupboard. Elizabeth, more gullible than John, tended to believe her, while John did not, and a noisy argument would ensue.

Despite the teasing Elizabeth and John were inseparable. They invented their own pastimes, some of which reflected a marked religious awareness. Safely hidden from adult eyes, the children procured an oblong tin, which they filled with apples and decorated with tiny home-made wax candles, using darning wool for wicks. This was carried to a private place, hidden by the low branches of a yew tree. Here they conducted their 'liturgy', after which they ate the apples.

The daily routine was sometimes varied with a children's party. During her early years Elizabeth lacked social confidence, disliking her appearance and regretting her 'mousy' hair, which was neither dark nor fair. She did not know many of her cousins, so when she went to a party given by the Debenhams in Kensington she was miserable. The Debenham children had prepared an entertainment in which the pretty, red-headed Alison played the part of a princess and captivated the visitors.[5] At teatime there was great competition to sit beside 'the princess'; to her surprise Elizabeth managed to gain the coveted seat and from that moment on became confident of her ability to achieve anything if she wanted it sufficiently.

Occasionally Elizabeth and John were invited to stay with their relations. Shortly after war was declared in 1914, Elizabeth, aged eight, and John, seven, were staying on their own with their father's sister, Nell Parker-Gray, in Northampton. During this visit news was received that their aunt's nephew, Hugh Barnes, had been killed; the two children responded to the unbearable tension that followed the announcement by giggling hysterically, a natural but embarrassing reaction that Elizabeth has never forgotten.

Apart from the death of this one cousin, the first World War seems to have had little effect on Elizabeth's daily life, although like everyone else she was affected by food shortages. When Zeppelin raids became sufficiently serious to send the family into the cellar, Elizabeth's curiosity outweighed her fear; she was excited rather than frightened and almost exhilarated by the sight of a Zeppelin crashing to the ground in flames.

Elizabeth had to wait until she was six to start school, as her parents wanted John to be able to start at the same time and he had to be five before the school would accept him. The two children attended Miss Newth's preparatory school in Baker Street.[6] By this time Elizabeth was reading fluently, having been taught by her mother, and for some time she had been making up fairy stories, which she had persuaded her mother to write down for her before she was capable of doing so for herself. Mrs Harman took the early instruction of her children very seriously; wishing to teach them herself, she joined the Parents National Educational Union.[7] Mrs Harman was rewarded for her trouble by seeing Elizabeth and John do well when they arrived at Miss Newth's.

In addition to their school classes, the children attended a gymnastics and dancing class run by a Miss Bretell, who also took them to the Marylebone Baths for swimming lessons. To start with, Elizabeth was among the 'push and struggle brigade' who could do no more than fling themselves from the steps as they attempted to splash their way across the width of the pool, but she was ambitious and determined and she soon became competent. Swimming, especially in the sea, was to become one of her greatest pleasures.

Elizabeth and John received their religious education from their mother, who instructed them in their Unitarian faith. From their earliest years she had read Gospel stories to them, carefully stressing that Jesus was a good man but that he was not God and was by no means perfect. Had he not run away from his parents, causing them sorrow? In her memoirs written over sixty years later, Elizabeth recalls her mother's low, serious and beautiful voice, which 'made me feel everything she said must be true' (*The Pebbled Shore*, p. 12). She also remembers her mother teaching her the 'Our Father' beside the lake in the Regents Park botanical gardens. The child adored her mother and greatly looked forward to her nightly visit to the nursery when she would sit on the end of Elizabeth's bed to hear her night prayers: 'Please God bless me and keep me safe this night. Bless Mother, Father, John . . .' (*The Pebbled Shore*, p. 12). The list lengthened as the babies arrived.

In the nursery grace was said before meals – Nurse Robins was an Anglican – but this custom was not followed by the Harman parents. Religious rites were of the simplest in Harley Street and generally restricted to the children's night prayers. This could be a source of embarrassment for the children when staying with their Harman cousins as they had no idea what was expected of them. On the occasion of their visit to Aunt Nell Parker-Gray, during which they received news of the death of cousin Hugh Barnes, seven-year-old John was asked to say grace before lunch. The child painstakingly learnt the formula but forgot to add the concluding 'Amen', which was the signal for the meal to proceed. One of the adults came to the rescue, but the children never forgot the frozen silence that followed John's lapse of memory.

In Harley Street Sundays were rigorously observed and, as there was no Unitarian church within easy reach, the family walked to a Congregational church. They attended the King's Weigh House in Duke Street until the introduction of High Church practices made the service unacceptable to them as Unitarians, when they transferred to the more distant Essex Unitarian church, near Notting Hill. Here Elizabeth found the prayers gloomy and the sermons long: she whiled away the time by 'shooting' rubber bands at the backs of the family in front. The older children were allowed to bring suitable books, which Elizabeth and Kitty slipped into their Sunday fur muffs. The younger ones were taken home by their mother before the thirty-minute sermon, and after the service Elizabeth, John and Kitty walked home with their father through Hyde Park to Harley Street. It was a long tramp, not altogether enlivened by his instructions on such topics as the Russian Revolution of 1917 or the 1919 Amritsar massacre in northern India; by the time they arrived home, they were tired and eager for lunch.

Sunday lunch was a formal occasion; the younger children remained upstairs in the care of Nurse Robins until they were old enough to cut up their own food and behave with decorum, which Elizabeth and John themselves often failed to achieve. They were frequently sent out of the dining room for bad behaviour. Once the meal had ended, the adults relaxed. The table was cleared, the cloth removed and the youngest child carried in to be wrapped in the undercloth and shot from one end of the polished table to the other amid squeals of joy.

After lunch came the ritual of distributing pocket money. The rate was two pennies for the older children, one penny for the younger ones, but pocket money had to be earned by the faultless recitation of verses from *Palgrave's Golden Treasury*. In the Harman household the Protestant work ethic, a fundamental tenet of Unitarian practice, was never relaxed. The purpose of life was work rather than enjoyment. Once the recitations were ended Mrs Harman often read Gospel stories to the children, or as a treat they might be taken to the London Zoo, which was then reserved for members only on Sundays.[8]

Sunday was the one day in the week when Mr Harman relaxed enough to devote an hour to his children. They played the 'Lion' game with him; Mr Harman closed his eyes and sat near the table, leaving a gap through which the children tried to pass without being caught by him. The penalty for being caught was a merciless tickling and for once their father tolerated their noisy cries. He also allowed them to let off steam by romping up and down the long passage to the front door, until they were exhausted and it was bedtime. Before going upstairs each child was allowed to ask their father to draw a picture of anything they chose. Mr Harman was a talented draughtsman and water-colourist but, ever thrifty, he drew the children's pictures on the backs of used envelopes or scraps of paper. Elizabeth, from the age of eight when the youngest child, Michael, was born, invariably asked her father to draw the birth of a baby. Nat Harman produced storks carrying bundles, doctors bearing black bags and tadpoles emerging from frog-spawn but never the birth of a child. The topic exercised a fascination for Elizabeth, but neither of her parents was prepared to discuss it. John, who was to become a Harley Street physician, was, however, able to inform his sister that a male and a female were necessary for the production of babies.

John discovered this information by observing the moths of silkworms that he and Elizabeth kept in a box on the nursery window-sill until they fell off and came to a sticky end on the balcony below. There, to Elizabeth's surprise, they oozed yellow fluid rather than red gore. In partnership with John she had also acquired a pair of newts and a budgerigar, but none survived. She had always been fascinated by living creatures and for a short time had hopes of having her own zoo in the Harley Street attics, but this did not materialise.

Elizabeth's early years were secure and happy, if somewhat regimented. The restrictions eased in 1913 when Mr Harman rented Lynchfield, in the village of Detling, near Maidstone, Kent. From then on the Harmans spent all the school holidays at Lynchfield, and it is the place to which Elizabeth looks back as the greatest source of happiness in her childhood. The house stood in a large garden, which provided endless delight. There were a croquet lawn, summer-house, barn, pergola and romantic, ivy-covered cave. They often played croquet, 'tag', 'rescue' and 'shipwreck' and sometimes their parents could be persuaded to join them.

The children often divided into pairs. Elizabeth and Kitty amused themselves by making booklets of pious texts, or took turns to preach sermons to each other. They played duets on the piano, quarrelling over which of them should have the more interesting treble part. Roger and Michael spent hours creating an elaborate dwelling between the front porch and the coach-house. When the boys had thatched and furnished it, they entertained the rest of the family there. Beyond the garden lay the North Downs, where the Pilgrim's Way, running from Winchester to Canterbury, and the river Medway invited exploration. As they grew older Elizabeth and John were allowed to venture further afield and when they were twelve and eleven respectively they followed part of the Pilgrim's Way on their bikes. In places this was a barely distinguishable muddy track across ploughed fields. The children fell off several times and were so dirty and dishevelled when they finally reached Canterbury Cathedral that they were turned away by an indignant verger.

Elizabeth has a clear memory of a family expedition on the river, which stands out as the only occasion on which she can recall being allowed to laugh at her father. Nat Harman missed his footing on the river bank and fell fully clothed into the water; to everyone's relief he was amused by his mishap, so his children were able to give vent to the laughter that they had attempted to suppress.

Lynchfield's only disadvantage was its size. There was only one living room and Mr Harman insisted on total silence when he was reading after dinner. Elizabeth disliked this tyranny but as she had always been fascinated by books herself, the silence presented no real hardship. In Harley Street she always read all the magazines that were put out for the patients and at the age of eleven, finding herself without a book, she trespassed into her father's consulting room where she discovered, among the many dull tomes on eye disease, *Staying the Plague*. The book, written by her father, was a scientific account of ways in which venereal disease could be prevented. Elizabeth read the book in secret from cover to cover and to some extent it satisfied her curiosity about sex.

Mrs Harman continued to read aloud to the family as they began to enter adolescence. Alexander Pope's translation of *The Iliad* made a great impression on Elizabeth, confirming a bias in favour of the underdog, which has remained with her. She sided with the defeated Trojans and would not abandon them, despite the pressure both John and her mother exerted in order to persuade her to support the Greeks. Although Mr Harman did not read to the children, he was quick to correct any careless use of English. If Elizabeth was so foolish as to declare an object 'frightful', he would ask, 'in what respect does it frighten you?'. He was equally exacting regarding the difference between 'will not' and 'can not'.

Idyllic as Lynchfield was, not all Elizabeth's memories are happy; it was at Lynchfield when she was twelve that she witnessed a rare quarrel between her parents, which convinced her that they were on the point of divorce. She was badly shaken and not easily reassured by her mother. On another occasion she so provoked her father that he struck her; the child exploited his loss of control with a fit of exaggerated weeping and again it was Mrs Harman who made peace between father and daughter. Possibly the most unpleasant experience of Elizabeth's childhood also took place during the holidays at Lynchfield. The family had spent the day at the seaside and Elizabeth, mistaking her parents' bathing hut for her own, blundered in on them. Her father roared at her to get out. She retreated 'in terror and confusion feeling that I had only just missed seeing something extremely nasty in the woodshed' (*The Pebbled Shore*, p. 5).

Occasionally Elizabeth would be invited to Abersoch, near Pwllheli in Wales, to stay for a holiday with her Nettlefold cousins on the Chamberlain side. Much as she enjoyed the sea, she was reluctant to be away from Lynchfield, which assumed greater importance after 1916. In that year Elizabeth and John left Miss Newth's and, being at separate schools, saw a great deal less of each other. At first Elizabeth was sent to a small non-conformist school in north London, where she was miserable. She was a 'swot', which made her unpopular with the other girls; she disliked the frequent games periods on Hampstead Heath and was tired out by the long bus journeys from Harley Street each day. Most of her former school friends had gone to the Francis Holland Church of England School for Girls in Baker Street and Elizabeth was determined to join them. She told her parents that she was so tired at the end of the day that she was always falling asleep and missing her bus stop. Surprisingly, they agreed to the change and in January 1916 Elizabeth transferred to the Francis Holland School.

There she worked hard and took an enthusiastic part in school activities. She acted in school productions of 'The Pied Piper' and 'Little Red Riding Hood', enjoying them so much that she told her mother that she was going to be an actress. Mrs Harman quashed her ambition, saying, 'I was much better at acting than you are, dear, but I was not good enough to be a professional' (*The Pebbled Shore*, p. 51). One of the school's commitments at that time was supporting the Lady Margaret

Hall Settlement in Lambeth.[9] The younger children were asked to bring toys for the poor children in Lambeth; Elizabeth found one or two discarded toys in the nursery cupboard, which she added to the school's collection. The children were also asked to bring comforts for the British prisoners of war in Germany. Elizabeth, being a conscientious child, took all these requests seriously. Apart from mathematics, with which she has always had to struggle, academic work came easily to her.

She also excelled at drawing and was put in for a public examination. A few hours before the examination Elizabeth was struck for the first time by migraine, which severely affected both her speech and her vision. The teachers had no idea what was wrong and in some alarm contacted Mr Harman; he made light of their concern, assuring them that Elizabeth had nothing worse than a migraine, from which he also suffered. He told them that she would be all right if allowed to rest, which she did, and by the afternoon she had recovered sufficiently to take the examination. Not surprisingly her results were below expectation. She arrived home shaken by the experiences of the day, but her father made no reference to what had happened, nor did he tell her that he, too, had migraines and that she was likely to suffer further attacks. Elizabeth has been plagued by migraines all her life, despite attempting various cures, but fortunately they were never again to interfere with an examination.

The child's undoubted intelligence became more obvious in 1920 when, at the age of fourteen, she moved to Headington, a small boarding school recently founded on the outskirts of Oxford. This change contributed substantially to the expansion of her previously restricted world. Mr Harman sent his sons to Oundle and Cambridge, but did not think that education was important for girls; fortunately for Elizabeth and Kitty, Mrs Harman thought otherwise and insisted that her daughters should have a good education and, if they wished, attend university.

Two of Elizabeth's Chamberlain cousins, Marian Beesly (the

daughter of Arthur Chamberlain's third daughter, Nellie) and Valerie Nettlefold, were already at Headington, and Aunt Maggie Nettlefold (Arthur Chamberlain's eldest daughter) used to invite Elizabeth to spend half-terms at their Queen Anne Manor in the Cotswolds. On these occasions she introduced Elizabeth to the delights of fine wine, Cotswold churches and village gossip. At school extra-curricular activities included visits to the Oxford Playhouse and opportunities to attend choral evensong or performances by the Bach Choir.

In 1922, when Elizabeth was fifteen, she gained the School Certificate with six credits, achieving the best results at her school. Always ambitious, she had been snubbed by her history mistress for producing a twelve-page essay on Parliament in Latin, but this had not cramped her efforts. At the final prize-giving she walked away with the school Essay prize as well as prizes for History, Architectural Drawing and Original Work. John teased her for being a 'disgusting pot-hunter'. Elizabeth's interest in art had been increasing. The prize-winning 'original work' was the painted scenery she had produced for the school production of *Dr Faustus*. There seemed to be every possibility that she could go on to study at the Slade School of Fine Art, but Elizabeth had her sights set on a scholarship to read English at Lady Margaret Hall, Oxford.

Elizabeth was now becoming impatient to move into the adult world. In 1923 when she was sixteen her mother gave her a modest monthly allowance, which enabled her to buy her own shoes, stockings and handkerchiefs, while Mrs Harman continued to choose the rest of her clothes. Without any reference to Elizabeth, she selected the shell-pink taffeta dress, frilled at the neck, sleeves and hem, in which Elizabeth attended her first teenage dance. Elizabeth accepted her mother's choice placidly, but Kitty was furious, claiming that pink was *her* colour. The day after the dance Elizabeth went down with a raging attack of 'flu, which may explain why the dance made little impression on her.

Elizabeth's maiden aunt Mary Chamberlain understood Elizabeth's impatience for greater independence. A few months before the Lady Margaret Hall scholarship examination she decided to take her niece on holiday for two weeks in the Haute Savoie. Elizabeth kept a diary from which it is clear that she revelled in this first experience of 'abroad'. She wrote lyrically of the Alpine scenery, sketched endlessly in the small village of Pralognan, where they were staying, and delighted in the companionship of her aunt. Aunt Mary gave Elizabeth tips on sketching, offered comfort when she sprained a wretchedly weak ankle and encouraged her in her attempts to enter the grown-up world. Mr Harman was prepared to acknowledge that Elizabeth was no longer a child to the extent of allowing her to put her hair up, although the style had gone out of fashion. She wound her long plaits into coils round her ears, although her contemporaries, the 'flappers', were all bobbing their hair. Her father refused to allow her to cut her hair and still less to wear make-up. One day when he met her leaving the house wearing 'Tangee' lipstick, a lipstick so discreet as to be almost invisible, he told her that she looked like a tart, and marched her back into the house to remove it. Eventually Mrs Harman persuaded her husband to allow Elizabeth to have the longed-for bob, but she could not persuade him to change his views on make-up.

In dealing with Elizabeth's increasing maturity, Mrs Harman's approach was subtler and more successful. She disapproved of smoking, but rather than issuing a direct prohibition she offered a bribe: Elizabeth, then aged eighteen, was promised £25 if she neither smoked nor drank alcohol before she was twenty-one. She observed the ban until she was twenty after which she smoked and drank freely. However, having abstained for two years, she successfully asked for part-payment.

In the Haute Savoie, however, Elizabeth was far from parental strictures. The only sour note in her generally appreciative diary was provoked by her ingrained hostility to the

Roman Catholic Church. Reared in a tangibly Protestant household, with prejudices reinforced by such books as Charles Reade's *The Cloister and the Hearth* and Charles Kingsley's *Westward Ho!*, she was scathing about 'RC gimcrack finery' and about Catholic shrines or chapels, such as the 'side altar of a mountain chapel, [where] slung on a wire was a unique collection of old crutches, walking sticks etcetera' (*Diary*, 23rd July 1924). Such criticism stands out starkly against her general delight in all that she saw and everyone she met, from the village urchins to the hotel waiters.

On this holiday it also became evident that Elizabeth herself was becoming increasingly attractive to the opposite sex. One of the guides who led them into the mountains was clearly smitten; he gathered posies of wild flowers for Elizabeth and when they stopped to rest laid out his raincoat for her to sit on. A young artist who was staying at the same hotel, Hugh Johnson, was also seriously attracted. On his return to England he went to visit Mr Harman to request his daughter's hand in marriage. Hardly surprisingly, the request was refused. Elizabeth, who had regarded the episode as no more than a mild flirtation, was not told of this first proposal of marriage until many years later.

After the holiday Elizabeth returned to Headington to prepare for the scholarship examination. She had always been a hard worker and in this last term, when she was seventeen, she kept a detailed commonplace book with 'E HARMAN : PRIVATE' scratched on the black cover. The pages are filled with quotations, analyses, criticism and personal reactions to events and people. Her taste was catholic; it embraced the Greek dramatists and the Latin poets and ranged from William Shakespeare to Rupert Brooke, from William Hazlitt to John Buchan. She noted every book that she read, every play and every concert that she attended. Elizabeth's commonplace book also contains original work. She had already tried her hand at a story of the French Revolution, which she called 'On the

Stroke of Twelve'. Her mother, to whom she showed all her work, dismissed this attempt for containing, 'too much talk, not enough action'.

In 1924, at seventeen, she was more successful with lyrical verse, a sample of which she submitted to a competition organised by the Girl Guide Association. The poet Alfred Noyes placed her sixth among the ten adult finalists. Elizabeth was also successful with 'a six-line warning in verse' for the *Spectator*. In 'The Moving Staircase' she described the fate of John, who failed to step off the escalator right foot first:

> The stairs were badly out of gear all day
> John reappeared at intervals, they say.

Elizabeth was then at the top of the school, but there were only two girls in the Sixth Form and she was the only one studying English. Unfortunately her teacher knew little about the scholarship papers and was accompanied everywhere by a Pekinese, which frequently disrupted lessons. Elizabeth consequently failed to gain the coveted place and was not even given an interview. The school seems to have realised that the fault did not lie with Elizabeth. After her unexpected failure fully qualified staff were appointed and the Sixth Form was expanded.

On Elizabeth, however, the effect of failure was less positive. Closing her mind to academic study, she flung herself into a round of social activities, staying with friends and relations, accompanying her parents to parties and falling in love with a young doctor from Maidstone who was one of her father's students. This young man also wanted to marry her; he put the request to Elizabeth rather than to her father, but she was still only eighteen and was not prepared to commit herself.

In the summer of 1925 Dr Bertrand Dawson, another Harley Street physician, whose daughter had just returned from studying at Grenoble university, suggested that Elizabeth take a six-month course in French there.[10] Lodgings were found in a small village above the town, which were let to students by Madame Besson, a war widow. Madame Besson immediately took to Elizabeth 'because she was so orderly'. This marked a radical change: not long before, Mrs Harman had told Elizabeth that she found it hard to love someone who was so untidy!

After a brief bout of homesickness Elizabeth began to revel in her new-found independence, although her father continued to exercise his authority. When he managed to put a stop to her wandering through Grenoble alone, she found a Dutch student to accompany her. The two believed themselves to be in love and corresponded briefly after leaving Grenoble, although the romance soon fizzled out. Another of Madame Besson's lodgers was Robert Mathew. Robert was a Catholic, but Elizabeth was prepared to overlook this on account of his intriguing eccentricity. Robert never went to lectures and in cold weather never left his bed! Many years later, his cousin, the Dominican priest Gervase Mathew, was to be responsible for Elizabeth's instruction in the Catholic faith.[11]

In March 1925, after six months of study interspersed with dances and skiing expeditions, Elizabeth returned to London with her ambition for Oxford rekindled. For this second attempt to gain a scholarship she found an Oxford graduate to coach her. In the eight months between her return and the examination, she spent her time studying and attending any relevant public lecture she could find. The hard work paid off. On 18th December 1925 *The Times* listed the Lady Margaret Hall scholarship awards in order of merit. Elizabeth Harman was the second name on the list. Her tutors said later they could hardly believe that she was the same candidate who had failed so miserably in the previous year. Her parents, proud and delighted, gave her a silver tankard, which still adorns her mantelpiece in Chelsea.

Elizabeth had a further nine months to fill before the start of the university year in October 1926. Her mother persuaded her to undertake voluntary work for the Unitarian church. The church ran a thrift scheme for the slum-dwellers in Lisson Grove, which was within walking distance of Harley Street. Every week Elizabeth collected small sums from any household that could be persuaded to join the weekly savings scheme; however, she never went inside the houses and her contact with the families who lived there was minimal.

During these months Elizabeth had other concerns. Although in earlier years she had been content to allow her mother to choose her dance dresses, she had now become intensely interested in her clothes and appearance. She compared herself unfavourably with her mother, with her dark eyes and rosy cheeks. She was of larger build and had yet to lose her puppy fat. She was only too aware that her landlady in Grenoble, Madame Besson, had once described her as 'colossally fat'. She embarked on a radical diet and managed to drop from nine stone to seven, thereby damaging her health to the point when her monthly periods ceased. Scared by this development, she confided in her mother, who, having satisfied herself that Elizabeth was not pregnant, consulted her husband. Mr Harman's remedy was simple. Elizabeth must eat more. Her weight increased to eight and a half stone, and she has generally been able to keep it at that. One final change completed her preparations for Oxford. She told her friends and family that in future she would prefer to be known by her full name Elizabeth, rather than the diminutive 'Betty'.

The 'new' Elizabeth, slender and vivacious, who in later years would look as good as her adult daughters in a mini-skirt, surprisingly lacked confidence in her appearance. She had a broad brow, regular features and a ready smile that began with her eyes; yet she disliked her brown hair, pallid complexion and even her eloquent eyes, regretting that their colour hovered between grey and blue. What she could not know was that her greatest charm lay in her enthusiasm, which lit her whole being with a glow that was to prove irresistibly infectious.

2

Oxford at her Feet

Elizabeth decided to go to Oxford alone. She was aware that she had reached a turning-point and wanted to savour it without distraction. At Lady Margaret Hall, generally referred to as LMH, she was assigned a cold, dark room in the original and hideous Victorian 'Old Hall'. There was no radiator, the coal fire threw out little heat and the lights had been wired to prevent the simultaneous use of overhead light and reading lamp. Elizabeth quickly solved this problem with a bronze hair-pin, which, when applied to the light switch, enabled both lights to be switched on. She was accustomed to the cold and regarded it as trivial compared to the luxury of having a room to herself: at home she and Kitty always had to share. The only necessity she lacked was a comfortable chair in which to work. For thirty shillings (£1.50) she acquired a wooden chair with an adjustable back and arms broad enough to balance a cup and saucer. This proved so satisfactory that she has used it ever since.[1]

Elizabeth had the good fortune to go to Oxford in the late 1920s, a 'golden age'. She found herself part of a glittering set, many of whose members were later to make their names. Among them were the poets John Betjeman and Stephen Spender, the historian David Cecil and the classicist Maurice Bowra, the cartoonist Osbert Lancaster and the actress Margaret Rawlings. There were also future politicians, including Hugh Gaitskell, who was to lead the Labour Party. Generally women undergraduates were at a disadvantage at this time; neither brains nor beauty guaranteed an entrée into the charmed circle of Oxford men, who tended to seek female companionship among either the London debutantes or the local prostitutes. A few fortunate girls had a brother or cousin who was prepared to introduce them to their own men friends, and Elizabeth was among their number. One of her Chamberlain cousins, Michael Hope, had preceded her to Oxford and when she arrived he was in his second year at Christ Church studying Greats, otherwise known as Literae Humaniores, which included the study of Greek, Latin, Philosophy and Ancient History. Michael offered to teach her to play golf and, while she was not a very promising pupil, they saw a great deal of each other, with the result that Michael fell 'head over heels in love' with her. He proposed and although he was refused this was never to cast a cloud over their lifelong friendship.

By her second term Elizabeth had become disenchanted with the English school. She was quick to make the decision that as a course of study English was second-rate and therefore could never satisfy her ambition to excel. She found the study of Anglo-Saxon an unrewarding chore and did not get on with her English tutor. While she was in the throes of this dis-satisfaction, Elizabeth was introduced to Maurice Bowra, who fuelled her enthusiasm for Greats. Needing her parents' consent to change courses, she sent off a long and impassioned letter to her mother, which demanded, 'answer by return, giving consent ... English has proved a wash-out. Greats is THE school at Oxford ... all the good men read it and few few girls. As I do not know the Greek alphabet, I shall have to stay up one extra year ... but once on Greats I shall get all the best tutors and lectures. Please answer at once per pc' (11th March 1927). Her parents agreed and by the time Elizabeth returned home for the spring vacation of 1927, she had changed from English to Greats.

In general, male undergraduates of the 1920s could be

divided into two 'camps', although the division was by no means hard and fast. 'Hearties were good college men who rowed in the college boat, ate in the college hall and drank beer and shouted'. The aesthetes, on the other hand, the set to which Gaitskell belonged, 'let their hair grow long . . . and never found out where the college playing fields were'.[2] (There were, of course, some men to whom neither description applied.) Among the aesthetes many were homosexual, although for a number this was no more than a passing phase. Gaitskell was not a homosexual himself, but he was not prepared to enter into a relationship with anyone who might disapprove of his friends who were so inclined.

Elizabeth's change of direction owed a certain amount to Hugh Gaitskell whom she had met in the spring term of 1927. They went for a walk and while sitting under a haystack he suddenly and solemnly asked Elizabeth what she thought of Oscar Wilde 'and all that'. 'Oscar Wilde?' she repeated. 'Oh, I think that's quite all right.' 'I'm so glad,' said Hugh fervently. 'If you hadn't thought that way we couldn't have gone on' (*The Pebbled Shore*, p. 48).

Their relationship was based on common intellectual interests. Hugh enjoyed Elizabeth's company and found her conversation delightful. For her part Elizabeth was captivated by the combination of intellectual ability and sophisticated charm. In those early days Hugh took it upon himself to direct Elizabeth's life: her reading, the part she played in college life, even her clothes were subjected to his forceful opinions.

Although Elizabeth ignored Hugh's strictures on her clothes, she allowed him to direct her reading and even struggled through Proust in French, translating it word by word, but failing to comprehend the whole. Hugh told her that she had such a lot on her side, she ought to make more of it. She should break away from the high-school atmosphere of both college and her girlfriends. Despite her devotion to Hugh, Elizabeth remained her own woman, assuming a leading role in some college activities, but avoiding others. She played a major part in all the college dramatic productions, and also swam for LMH in 'Dames' Delight', the boarded-off section of the river Cherwell, which was reserved for women. On the other hand she never set foot in the college chapel, seldom went into the undergraduate's Junior Common Room and rarely dined formally in hall.

It was Hugh who introduced Elizabeth to Maurice Bowra, Dean and later Warden of Wadham College. Elizabeth was spellbound by Bowra's personality: 'Voltaire and the Sun King rolled into one' (*The Pebbled Shore*, p. 63). Bowra lectured in classics and his rooms were the focal point for those studying classics and poetry. He was thought to be homosexual. His wit was renowned, his cruel barbs were generally tolerated and his dinner parties were famous although few women were invited.

Before returning to Oxford for the summer term of 1927 Hugh Gaitskell proposed to Elizabeth – but only as a matter of convenience: 'Of course it won't mean anything,' he explained, 'just so that we would be free to see each other without people interfering' (*The Pebbled Shore*, p. 56). In the light of a later comment made in a letter to her, the proposal seems to have been a suggestion that they sleep together rather than a commitment to marry, but whatever Hugh's intention, Elizabeth declined his offer. She had no intention of entering into a sexual relationship outside marriage and she was enjoying herself too much with her many friends to think seriously of a permanent commitment.

It can happen that the most popular girl with men is the least popular with women. This does not seem to have been the case with Elizabeth, who also had numerous women friends. Among them was Armorel Heron-Allen, a strikingly beautiful zoologist, and Audrey Townsend, a scholar, reading history. Both arrived at Lady Margaret Hall at the same time as Elizabeth and it was Audrey who had introduced Elizabeth to Hugh, who was her cousin.

Hugh's proposal and Elizabeth's refusal left their relationship unchanged and he invited her to the New College Ball in June at the end of the first year. This had been something of a triumph: she had changed her course of study, gained a group of brilliant friends and received two proposals of marriage.

While she was greatly looking forward to the New College Ball, she was less excited about the Magdalen Ball to which she went with a party of friends on the previous night. Little did she guess that the events of those two nights would shape the rest of her life. Towards the end of the Magdalen Ball Elizabeth encountered a recumbent figure draped over a chair, sound asleep. Drawn by the resplendent livery of the Bullingdon, that most exclusive of hunting clubs – navy-blue tailcoat, white facings and brass buttons, worn over a yellow waistcoat – Elizabeth was staggered as much by the 'monumental beauty of the figure' (*The Pebbled Shore*, p. 57) as by the stupidity of any girl who could abandon such a partner. She stood staring at the sleeping Frank Pakenham for a moment or two, before returning to her own party on the dance floor. Later she would learn of Frank's facility for sleeping: the moment he was horizontal he became dead to the world.

There was a repeat performance the following night at the New College Ball to which she went with Hugh, his elder brother Arthur and one or two others. Some time after midnight Hugh and Elizabeth left the dance floor to take a break and there again was Frank Pakenham stretched out, sound asleep. They all crowded round, while Elizabeth, egged on by her friends, and thinking of 'the sleeping beauty in reverse', planted a kiss on Frank's forehead. He half woke and opening his eyes saw Elizabeth bending over him. 'I'd like to kiss you, but I don't know how,' he mumbled and went straight back to sleep. Although at the time the incident seemed to have made little impression, neither Frank nor Elizabeth was to forget it.

The two were to meet again in London a few weeks later. Frank had gained a congratulatory first-class degree, securing an Alpha for every paper except Economics. To celebrate he invited his friends to a theatre party, preceded by dinner at the Café Royal. Hugh had been invited and Elizabeth accompanied him. Hugh and Frank were good friends, both were at New College, both had read Modern Greats (Politics, Philosophy and Economics) and for a time they had shared the same lodgings. In the event the party fell a little flat as Frank failed to reach the theatre. He had rounded off dinner by standing on a chair, doing a pirouette and passing out. The following day Elizabeth would have liked to discover whether or not her host had recovered, but felt diffident about telephoning. Sensing that he had a rival, Hugh dissuaded her, insisting that Pansy, one of Frank's four sisters, was looking after her brother and she should not fuss.

Over the next three years Elizabeth and Frank met only once, at one of those stilted Lady Margaret Hall tea parties which, by LMH rules, had to be held in certain designated common rooms and chaperoned by a don. Elizabeth had invited Frank but surprisingly he appeared to take no interest in her. In his autobiography *Born to Believe* Frank indicated that his attraction to Elizabeth lay behind his decision not to take a second degree in law at London, but to stay in Oxford for the first year of the degree.[3]

Elizabeth was totally unaware that she had aroused any interest in Frank and, although she had been struck by his looks and was impressed by his reputation for intelligence, her interest lay elsewhere. At the New College Ball she had danced most of the night with Arthur Gaitskell, Hugh's elder brother, who was home on leave from the Sudan where he worked in the civil service. He was taller and more debonair than Hugh and swept Elizabeth off her feet. The next day she took Arthur to Wytham Woods, a well-known trysting ground outside Oxford and later she invited him to a meal at Harley Street. She was sufficiently interested in Arthur to ask her mother's opinion of him. Mrs Harman, fearing that Elizabeth might throw over Oxford in order to marry Arthur, was not encouraging. She had no cause for concern; Arthur returned to the Sudan and their short correspondence soon petered out.

When in October 1926 Elizabeth returned to Oxford for her second year, Hugh had taken his degree and left Oxford. He had outgrown student life, in which Elizabeth was becoming increasingly immersed. Inevitably they drifted apart, but when they met later at a party of Maurice Bowra's in February 1928, their interest in one another was rekindled. The following summer Hugh made a final attempt to cement their relationship by inviting Elizabeth to join him for a sophisticated dinner party in Paris. Others, including Maurice Bowra, had been invited and many years later Elizabeth was astounded to discover from Philip Williams's biography of Hugh that he had intended to propose marriage to her on that evening.[4]

Elizabeth was never without admirers. One hapless young man let the air out of her bicycle tyres, planning to pass by as she struggled with the pump. When she found out she was furious and refused to speak to him again. During these years she became firm friends with David Cecil, who was then a young history don at Wadham. Another friend and admirer was Quintin Hogg, later to become Lord Hailsham,[5] who said of her that there was not an undergraduate in Oxford who would not have considered it a privilege to hold an umbrella over her head.[6]

In 1929 Quintin Hogg became President of the Oxford Union and was able to persuade his father, Lord Chancellor under the Conservative government of Stanley Baldwin, to speak at the Union summer debate. Quintin gave a large dinner at the Union beforehand to which he invited Elizabeth, now in her third year, paying her the compliment of placing her on the left of the Lord Chancellor. After dinner the men signed the visitors' book, indicating that the women should not follow suit. Elizabeth, in an early demonstration of feminism, signed, reasoning that if she could sit with men at the table, she could write her name alongside theirs. Many years later, when she had an opportunity to inspect the book, she found that her name had been expunged.

During her second year Elizabeth had been pleased to discover a new mentor in Maurice Bowra. In her third year (1928–9) she spent increasing amounts of time alone with him, often lunching in his white-panelled rooms at Wadham and constantly probing his mind. 'Why do the Greeks dominate all knowledge? Why are Greek writers so important? What is the point of all this study?' (*The Pebbled Shore*, p. 70). Bowra took all these questions seriously. Now and then, during the vacation, he sent her verses, and bought books for her – Yeats's *The Tower*, Robert Bridges's *Testament of Beauty* and Pindar's *Pythian Odes*, this last in his own translation in collaboration with H. T. Wade-Gery, a colleague at Wadham.[7] With hindsight, such attentions seem pointed enough, but not then to Elizabeth, who was overwhelmed when Bowra asked her to marry him. She fled from his rooms, barely managing to express coherent thanks and leaving his question unanswered. At this time, it must be acknowledged, Elizabeth was as self-centred as any young woman of her age, and it did not occur to her to consider Maurice Bowra's feelings. For months afterwards, glorying in the compliment she had been paid by the great Bowra, she floated around in an elated glow.

Oxford friends frequently took Elizabeth beyond the confines of the University. Harry d'Avigdor Goldsmid, the son of a committed Zionist, took her to his house in Kent where for the first time she came into contact with the Jewish community. Christine Willans, also at LMH, introduced her to her cousin Naomi Mitchison.[8] The radical Naomi was passionately interested in politics and awakened Elizabeth's interest in a world beyond Oxford, although politics as such were of little concern to her then. Armorel Heron-Allen's father gave a splendid twenty-first birthday party for his beautiful and brilliant daughter, who was tipped for a first-class degree, and as Armorel's closest friend Elizabeth was also the recipient of gifts from Mr Heron-Allen. She received three rare sixteenth-century volumes including Erasmus' *Colloquia*, which sparked an interest in the personalities of Tudor England that would later catch fire.

Elizabeth had come up to Oxford a few months after the ending of the General Strike of 1926. In her final year, 1929, the effects of the Wall Street crash reached the UK, increasing poverty and unemployment. Elizabeth and her friends, absorbed in their studies and their pursuit of pleasure, were oblivious to the wider world. Although she claimed that her poem 'Ode to the Muses', published in December 1929 by *Fritillary*, the magazine published by the Oxford women's colleges, was inspired by the Slump, it now seems heartless, not to say cynical:

> Shut up your singing
> Ain't got a sou,
> Take your little monkey faces
> Back to the zoo.
> Take your barrel-organs
> Back to the mews
> (And let's have a nibble at the peas in your shoes.)

Elizabeth was prominent in a number of societies, including the LMH Dramatic Society, Oxford University English Club and the Poetry Club, where she acted as secretary and first came in contact with Stephen Spender. Her work also appeared in other undergraduate magazines including *Cherwell* and *Isis*, which also chose her as an 'Isis Idol', observing, 'It is almost without precedent for a woman to be an Idol: but Miss Harman herself appears to be almost without precedent. Her career in the University has entitled her to such honour as we can give.'

Although Elizabeth never told her mother about the proposals of marriage from Hugh Gaitskell or Maurice Bowra,

Mrs Harman was sometimes anxious about the effect of the many distractions on her daughter's studies. Elizabeth had become something of a byword in the family and her mother was hardly reassured by a letter from one of her sisters-in-law, which said, 'I hear Nat's girl is the toast of Oxford'. Miss Grier, Elizabeth's Principal, who was known for her understanding attitude to students, was also becoming impatient with what she regarded as unseemly behaviour in a fourth-year student.

Elizabeth's credit in college finally ran out one evening when she returned at 11.30 p.m., fifteen minutes late.[9] She had, in fact, arrived on time at the gate, but her escorts, for whom there was no such time limit, had kept the party going and Elizabeth was unable to drag herself away. The porter reported Elizabeth, who found herself before an irate Miss Grier the following morning. 'So much noise outside the college . . . this is not the first time . . . The college may have to reconsider your future.' 'Everyone is expecting me to be sent down,' she wrote to her mother (20th October 1929).

Elizabeth nevertheless had her sights set on a first-class degree. She was a hard worker with the stamina to combine a hectic social life with serious study; regardless of the hour she went to bed, she was always up for breakfast in hall at 8 a.m. She worked at her books every day for five or six hours, a routine she has maintained throughout her life. With her final year upon her, Elizabeth resolved to abstain from all parties – which nevertheless did not preclude going out to dinner with a male friend.

In the summer of 1930 – her last term – Elizabeth found lodgings in Chadlington Road owned by a classicist who agreed to coach her. Despite this last-minute help, she was in such a panic the night before her finals that she barely slept and turned up for the first paper in a state of exhaustion. Although she enjoyed writing her examination papers, she had little confidence that they would gain her the coveted first. There remained one final and slender chance. An oral examination followed the marking of the written papers and it was not unknown for a borderline candidate to raise her class in a viva. Elizabeth's viva was two weeks off. Bored by an important period of Roman history when the state was dominated by the two worthy Gracchi brothers, she had avoided all questions on them, but, having a hunch that this topic would come up in the viva, decided to revise it thoroughly.[10]

Before embarking on this final revision there were farewell parties and celebrations. Elizabeth and Armorel held a large cocktail party at the Randolph Hotel, which was to be a celebration for Armorel, who had already gained her expected first, and also a farewell.[11] Afterwards Elizabeth and Armorel planned to spend a week in Devon with friends in the holiday house belonging to one of Elizabeth's Chamberlain cousins. But fate intervened and tragedy put an end to their plans.

On the way to Devon the car in which Armorel was driving went off the road. Armorel was killed immediately, while her fiancé, Patrick de Laszlo, escaped with minor injuries. He and Armorel's family were left devastated, and Elizabeth was plunged into her first experience of bereavement. Everyone was very kind to Elizabeth, but the only person who could have helped was Armorel herself. She felt that she would only come to life again if she could discuss the whole affair with Armorel (*The Pebbled Shore*, p. 93). Elizabeth was inconsolable and found herself unable to concentrate. The viva, her last chance of a first, was little more than a week away and yet she could not bring herself to open her books. Did it really matter? Armorel had got a first and little good had it done her.

Elizabeth's hunch about the Gracchi had proved correct. The examiners spent forty minutes questioning her on the two brothers in a genuine attempt to help her to amplify what she had written and secure a first, but she was unable to add to what she had originally written, although she learnt later that the rest of her papers were good.

3

Approaching Marriage

Elizabeth received numerous letters commiserating with her on missing the first. They brought some comfort and gradually, as the shock of bereavement began to subside, she was able to turn her mind to the problem of her own future. Then, astonishingly, in July 1930, Frank Pakenham arrived unannounced on the doorstep. Elizabeth had seen him once in the last three years but had attached little importance to the meeting.

Frank had been invited by friends to spend a weekend in Oxford and had spent the night dreaming of Elizabeth; he had had no idea of where he would find her, but had dreamt that she was staying at a house in Chadlington Road. Following his dream he turned up on her doorstep. Elizabeth's reaction to her unexpected visitor was all that Frank could have hoped for: '... I had an overpowering but inexplicable conviction that something unalterable had been mapped for the future ...' (*The Pebbled Shore*, p. 96). The immediate purpose of his visit was to invite Elizabeth to stay with his family at Pakenham, in Ireland, and also to suggest that she should join himself and his friend Evan Durbin at Balliol during the first week in August, where they were acting as tutors at the Workers Educational Association summer school.[1] Coincidentally, and unbeknown to Frank, lecturing for the WEA had already been suggested to Elizabeth as a career possibility.

The kiss that had half woken him three years earlier had

33

prompted Frank into inviting Elizabeth to the Café Royal. It had also induced him to stay in Oxford rather than go to London. Since then, however, to all outward appearances Elizabeth had had no place in Frank's life.

Frank Pakenham was the second son of the fifth earl of Longford who had been killed in 1915 fighting courageously at Gallipoli. His mother had never hidden her preference for Edward, her elder son, who was now the sixth earl, and had thus severely undermined Frank's confidence. Having acquired a congratulatory first in Politics, Philosophy and Economics at Oxford, Frank had failed to complete his law studies and also lost a significant portion of his small patrimony on the stock market.

Although as a student Frank had been to some extent protected from the harsher realities of poverty and unemployment, he had never lost touch with the Eton Manor Boys' Club at Hackney Wick.[2] Thus while enjoying weekend house parties in the company of 'bright young things', he was sufficiently dissatisfied with his life to take up his tutor's suggestion of working for the WEA. In 1929 he secured a permanent post as a WEA lecturer and he spent his first year in the post in Stoke-on-Trent, teaching students and living with a railwayman and his family.

Elizabeth, on the other hand, knew almost nothing about deprivation. Nevertheless, she took up Frank's suggestion to join him at the WEA summer school, where she found herself tutoring two girls from Lincoln on American expressionist drama and a third, Leah Grocott, from Longton in North Staffordshire, on Rousseau's 'social contract'.

Elizabeth adopted the WEA motto, 'learn as you teach', with considerable benefit to herself and Leah Grocott, who soon brought along one of her friends. To an extent Frank was able to fill in gaps in Elizabeth's knowledge of the social background of her students from his own experience of the North Staffordshire area, where the effects of the 1929 Slump – poverty, low wages and unemployment – were as severe as anywhere in England. The students were avid for knowledge and respected their teachers, but when it came to the practical challenges of daily life, both sides were aware that the roles were reversed. This fostered a camaraderie, which Elizabeth found almost as stimulating as the enthusiasm of her students. She understood their insatiable desire to learn and entered into their dreams and fears. Leah Grocott wanted Elizabeth to give a series of twelve lectures in the Potteries on literature and one of the Kent branches was also requesting that she lead a weekend school on 'The Financial Side of Unemployment'. Excited as she was by the idea, Elizabeth knew nothing of economics, and felt that she would have to turn down the Kent request.

Evan Durbin, lecturer at the London School of Economics, thought otherwise.[3] He insisted that he could teach her 'the whole of economics' over one lunch (*The Pebbled Shore*, p. 101). When this turned out to be over-ambitious, he suggested that she attend the LSE, where she could easily combine a degree course with a weekly lecture in North Staffordshire. Elizabeth was reluctant to embark on yet more years of study, but a letter to her parents (then in Canada on BMA business; 23rd August 1930) struck a positive note. Having described the 'enormous fun' of the WEA summer school at Balliol, she explained her plans for the WEA, in which Frank was already assuming significance. 'The idea is to arrange a weekly class every Friday, because on that day Frank will be having one on Economics.'

This letter was written a few days before her visit to Pakenham, the Longford seat, in county Westmeath.[4] Successive earls had extended and embellished the castle and by 1930 the castle with its dry moat, towers and battlements covered two acres. The estate, no less impressive, included a walled garden, glass-houses, park, farms and great lake. The castle was at that time the home of Frank's elder brother, Edward, and his wife Christine; the couple were in their twenties and were childless, as they were to remain. Edward was an eccentric, absorbed in a love for all things Irish, especially the Irish theatre, and a passionate supporter of an independent Irish nation. He had an uncontrollable addiction to food and eventually became massively overweight, dying of a stroke in 1961, at the age of fifty-eight.

Among Elizabeth's fellow guests on her first visit in the summer of 1930 were John Betjeman and Alastair Graham with his friend Evelyn Waugh. Frank, involved in a local tennis tournament, left Elizabeth to fish on the lake with Edward. One afternoon, when they had failed to raise a single bite, Elizabeth, who at this time professed no religious belief, took it into her head to challenge God to a proof of existence by demanding a catch. The answer was swift and abundant. The combined strength of both anglers was heavily taxed in landing a huge pike, which was itself stuffed with small fish. Elizabeth delighted in what she interpreted as a divine sense of humour, and the bizarre incident made a lasting impression on her then outwardly non-existent faith. Fishing was not the only diversion; on some days they crowded into Edward's car and went in search of ruined abbeys and deserted houses or Celtic crosses, around which John Betjeman and Edward conducted a quasi-religious rite. Another of Edward's sports was the 'hunting' of donkey-carts, which he loved to approach at full throttle with horn blaring, until the wretched driver got out of the way, usually by tumbling into the ditch.

Evelyn Waugh joined in all the tomfoolery, arranging tragi-farcical tableaux, which were photographed against the back-drop of the great nail-studded front door. In one of these photographs Elizabeth played a fainting damsel; in another Edward attacked Evelyn with a boot brush. In the evenings they sang, led by Edward who had a particular liking for Irish Protestant hymns. It was an unusual situation for the 1930s, in that no members of the older generation were present to insist on sobriety and order. Andrews, the Welsh non-conformist butler, seems to have been the only person who could restrain Edward.

Years later in her memoirs (*The Pebbled Shore*, p. 101) Elizabeth was to describe her first visit to Pakenham as eccentric, intellectual, high-spirited and comical: for herself and Frank it was also romantic. For many years Evelyn Waugh was critical of Elizabeth, claiming patronisingly that Frank had married beneath him. But on the final evening at Pakenham, as the guests were going upstairs to bed, Waugh made a point of waylaying Elizabeth and urging her to follow Frank to his bedroom.

She needed little encouragement; by the end of the holiday the premonition that had seized her on Frank's arrival in Chadlington Road had been excitingly confirmed. She had become convinced that Frank was 'her sort of man'. The two young people spent the last night at Pakenham sitting chastely on either side of Frank's huge double bed, talking endlessly. Neither then, nor on subsequent occasions before their marriage, did they sleep together, and both came to their wedding night as virgins. Frank was entranced by Elizabeth's looks and poise. To the amazement of all who knew his habit of keeping his clothes together with safety pins and his indifference to his appearance (a trait that he inherited from his father), on his return to London he bought himself a new hat. He had discovered 'Harmans', the hatters, in Bond Street; the shop had no connection with Elizabeth's family, but it pleased Frank to have her name inscribed on his hatband.

Given their differing social backgrounds and divergent interests, theirs was not an obvious match. Frank was a convinced Anglican, fanatical in his devotion to sport and already preparing himself for a political career as a Conservative. Elizabeth then had neither knowledge nor interest in politics, considered herself a humanist and was steeped in the literary arts. The only interest they shared was a passionate and classless concern for people, but what chance was there that two such strong-willed and divergent personalities could create a successful marriage on such meagre common ground?

Nevertheless, in the early days, despite Frank's diffidence, their courtship seemed to be advancing smoothly. Each spent six days a week in London, Frank at the newly formed Conservative Research Department (where he worked under Elizabeth's cousin, Neville Chamberlain), and Elizabeth at the London School of Economics. Both were teaching for the WEA in North Staffordshire and scheduled their lectures so that they could travel back to London together in the early hours of Saturday morning. Elizabeth made her base at the village of Meir, spending a night with the WEA district secretary Edmund (Ted) Hobson and his wife Maria. On Friday mornings she then took the local bus to Longton, where her lectures on modern American drama were a great success. Frank lodged with a Mrs Adams in Fenton, where he lectured in economics. On Friday evenings, with their tasks accomplished, they met at Frank's lodgings, where they were joined by a number of other WEA friends. The ensuing singsong around Mrs Adams's upright piano continued until midnight, when Elizabeth and Frank hurried off on foot to Stoke station to claim their sleepers on the 1.15 a.m. London Express.

Elizabeth was in no doubt that she loved and needed Frank, but Frank's situation was altogether more complicated, as he tried to explain in his frequent letters. While one letter insisted that 'he had never stopped thinking about her' (*The Pebbled Shore*, p. 109) and another insisted on his desire to be married to her, he had been so imbued with self-doubt that diffidence overshadowed his feelings. This lack of confidence was partly due to his position in his family. As the second son he had been conditioned to believe that his limited finances must make marriage unlikely, as he would be unable to support a wife and family. Even his brilliant first had done little to restore self-confidence, so radically undermined had it been by his mother, who had neither praised nor even noticed his efforts. His letters declared his devotion to Elizabeth, but were accompanied by self-accusations and gloomy self-analysis. The note attached to her Christmas present – a pearl bar brooch – was in typical vein: 'I don't think it particularly nice but I hope you will wear it' (*The Pebbled Shore*, p. 115).

Elizabeth wore the brooch, but in two poems written at this time her irritation is palpable. The first is dedicated 'To F. Inarticulate Unreliable Incapable of Endearments' (*The Pebbled Shore*, p. 110) and the second (ibid., p. 112) bears the title 'In Horror of Those who are Sadly Happy or Cheerfully Resigned'. Given Frank's lack of self-confidence, the semi-public situation of the London Express and the North Stafford Hotel in which they waited for it were unthreatening settings, in which he found it less difficult to express his feelings. On the bitterly cold night of 21st November 1930 Frank and Elizabeth had arrived at Stoke in good time for their train and were waiting as usual in the lounge of the hotel. There they were discovered by the manager in a close embrace. In high dudgeon he turned them out. Perhaps Frank's indignation encouraged him, for an hour or so later, at 2.15 a.m., on the London Express, he proposed to Elizabeth and was accepted.

Although Elizabeth had met several members of Frank's family, she had not yet met his mother, his grandmother or his sister Mary. Frank, on the other hand, had already been to dinner at Harley Street and met Elizabeth's parents. Shortly after the proposal he came to make a formal request for her hand and after dinner withdrew to the consulting room with Mr Harman. When they returned Frank looked 'pale and alarmed' (*The Pebbled Shore*, p. 111). Elizabeth knew that the interview had gone badly wrong and the two of them left as soon as possible. Elizabeth has never learnt what took place between Frank and her father, but it was clear that Frank's confidence had been further undermined, and that, despite the fact that he had proposed and been accepted by Elizabeth, he was now shying away from the whole idea of matrimony. In the following weeks he sank into a mood of impenetrable gloom. Totally baffled, Elizabeth took him to the consultant whom he had seen after he was concussed while riding in a point-to-point in 1928.[5] He made a second visit, unaccompanied by Elizabeth, but this was not a success. The consultant tried hypnosis, and Frank, having been asked to lie down and relax, fell fast asleep, as was his wont.

Elizabeth's cousin Michael Hope, who had proposed to her at Oxford, had now become engaged. He was a close friend but at first she could not bring herself to write a letter of congratulation. '. . . I was feeling so personally sore and worried . . . about [my own prospects of] marriage that I simply couldn't face seeing my bitterness on paper,' she explained when she finally wrote. Yet her certainty about her eventual marriage to Frank never seriously wavered.

They had intended to announce their engagement in *The Times* as soon as Frank had seen Elizabeth's father, but now the announcement had to be postponed indefinitely. This seemed to lessen the pressure on Frank, but it was an anomalous situation: their close friends and families knew that they intended to marry, but nothing could be said on the subject. A second visit to Pakenham raised their spirits. Frank, who is quintessentially Irish, never fails to be cheered by Ireland and once again they found themselves in a house party that included David Cecil and John Betjeman. Edward Longford was becoming increasingly involved with the Gate Theatre in Dublin and invited the whole company of actors to Pakenham one evening. They played charades and then the Truth Game. 'Who do you think is prettier, you or Elizabeth?' one of the Gate girls was asked. She replied, 'In England, Elizabeth, but here, me!'

Buoyed up by the visit and reluctant to accept Frank's gloomy view of his prospects, Elizabeth asked Frank about money. She was encouraged to learn that their combined incomes would come to more than £1000 – perfectly adequate for two people starting out on married life in the early 1930s. Each had a private income of £300 or so, and both were working – Frank's joint earnings from the Conservative Research Department and the WEA came to £600 a year, while Elizabeth's WEA salary was a modest £85.

In January 1931 Frank became secretary of a new Conservative research committee on the economy, which increasingly absorbed him. Elizabeth, therefore, found herself more isolated and decided to adjust her own focus. Instead of basing herself at her parents' house in London and spending one night in Stoke, she transferred her base to the Hobsons' council house in Meir, near Stoke, and returned to London one night a week for her tutorial at the LSE. 'Real life' in North Staffordshire held far more attraction than theoretical study in London, and her exposure to unemployment and poverty in Meir in the 1930s was to have a lifelong effect. She was deeply moved by the injustices in the lack of basic housing, nutrition and employment. Her indignation at the misery around her ended her indifference to politics and, inspired by Ted Hobson, who was an active member, she joined the Labour Party, to which she has given unwavering support ever since.

Although the decision to move further north was largely dictated by an instinct for self-preservation in the face of her difficulties with Frank, it became a fascinating and excellent foundation for Elizabeth's future political career. Her students were delighted with the move and benefited from her changed routine. She was able to extend her range of lectures to include Plato, asking provocatively, 'Should the good govern?'. In another series she traced the history of English drama and reached a splendid climax with an overview of the complementary arts of puppetry, masque and dance; she was steeped in literature and an excellent teacher, if less sure of her ground in economics.

In Stoke she was able to share the lives of her students to a far greater degree. While there was always enough to eat, Maria

Hobson could not afford lean meat or fresh fruit, and bread and potatoes were the constant fillers. Elizabeth gained a stone in weight. She found neither the environment nor the climate of the Potteries attractive, and in a letter to her parents written at the end of January 1931 she described a dull January day when she went for 'a long walk in some rather sooted and soaked country'. An expedition to the Birmingham Repertory Theatre to see the American play *See Naples and Die*, by the American dramatist Elmer Rice, was more entertaining. She managed to get a bed in Birmingham for herself and two of her students with one of her Chamberlain aunts, but while Aunt Bertha was quite willing to offer hospitality, she considered theatre tickets an unwarranted expense. Elizabeth held her ground, maintaining that such an outing would be remembered as a red-letter day.

She organised various activities. On one occasion the Oxford Labour Club came to Longton for a debate and on another she took a party of students on a weekend course at Barlaston Hall, Staffordshire, which had been presented to the WEA by the Wedgwood family. During that weekend the purpose of the WEA was admirably demonstrated by Eric Tams, a seventeen-year-old railway porter. Elizabeth offered Eric John Galsworthy's *Forsyte Saga* to read on the journey to Barlaston. Eric became oblivious to everybody around him as he read and the book opened up a whole new world. He mopped up all that the WEA had to offer and finally became the North Staffordshire area secretary.

In accordance with a request from the left-wing Social Democratic Federation, Elizabeth was also interviewing workers, union officials, teachers and local councillors. At the same time she was working on schemes for raising the school leaving age from fourteen to fifteen, as recommended by the Hadow Report of 1926.[6] This entailed visits to the various local schools from infant – her favourite age group – to elementary (then five to fourteen years). These projects were encouraged by her landlord, Ted Hobson, who was beginning to have ambitious plans for Elizabeth: she was only twenty-four, but he wanted to see her fighting the next election as a Labour candidate.

Ted arranged for Elizabeth to visit a coal-mine. She descended in the lift with the men and crawled along a conveyor 'that bristled with coal lumps' (*The Pebbled Shore*, p. 119) in order to reach the coal-face. She emerged elated but bruised and stiff, with one eye infected by coal-dust. She was indignant that the miners' so-called eight-hour day excluded the time required to reach the coal-face, which could take anything up to two hours and therefore added considerably to their working week. Ted also arranged for her to accompany the district nurse on her rounds. She saw for herself dangerous and broken stairs, roofs with gaping holes and damp, fungus-covered walls; the sight of a mother bathing her infant in a discarded food can seemed the epitome of deprivation and squalor.

Elizabeth also met local officials, Justices of the Peace, and the Member of Parliament for Hanley, Arthur Hollis. She made friends with the presidents of unions of pottery workers and of railway clerks, as well as the principals of several schools.

Shocked by the social conditions around her, Elizabeth became increasingly radical in her views and ever more critical of Ramsay Macdonald's minority Labour government, which had taken office in 1929 and seemed to be doing nothing to combat this deprivation. Frank in the meantime was being encouraged by his friends to stand as a Conservative candidate in a general election widely believed to be imminent, but his Conservative views were becoming less absolute. It was evident that Conservative economic policies had failed to deliver prosperity in the past, but he was far from convinced that the Labour policies of nationalisation and state control would do any better.

Frank was genuinely delighted when Elizabeth's name was put forward as a prospective Labour candidate for Stone and tentatively offered financial help, although politics was becoming an increasingly contentious issue between them. Frank was convinced that overproduction was the nub of the continuing economic problem, while Elizabeth believed it to be underconsumption. Moreover, Frank was nettled by Elizabeth's political independence. He was perfectly prepared to defer to her in matters of literature, and complied with her suggestions for making good the gaps in his knowledge of the English classics; but he expected Elizabeth to accept his word as law in matters of politics, whereas in fact she paid more heed to the views of her new friends in North Staffordshire.

At this time they were meeting only once a week, and their correspondence became almost acrimonious. 'What you don't realize is that I know a great deal about politics,' Frank wrote (*The Pebbled Shore*, p. 123). Elizabeth was unmoved; she was no longer prepared to be corrected by Frank or anyone else. Furthermore, she now believed that the paternalism advocated by Frank and the Conservatives was not merely ineffective but positively harmful to the workers. Did she not understand, he countered, 'that if the people could achieve everything for themselves, his own raison d'être as a politician – a member of the ruling classes – would disappear?' (*The Pebbled Shore*, p. 121).

Recriminating letters hurtled between London and Stoke from January 1931 until early in March, when Frank became ill and Elizabeth dropped everything in response to his summons. He had been troubled with rheumatic pains in his back for some time and had now collapsed in the train on his way home to visit his mother in Buckinghamshire. He was rushed to hospital where he was found to have pleurisy and bronchial pneumonia. 'I had to cut all my engagements,' Elizabeth wrote to her parents (23rd March), 'and help Frank to get home. He seemed as weak as water and he couldn't even carry a bag.' Elizabeth visited Frank every day at his London lodgings in Halsey Street, for at first his mother refused to allow him to be nursed at home; later she relented and took him in for a brief spell before finally sending him to a nursing home. There, with friends flocking round, he recovered sufficiently to begin convalescence at the Metropole Hotel in Brighton.

The experience of illness seems to have sharpened his appreciation of Elizabeth. 'You have been an angel,' he told her. 'But for you I would not be alive.' He was by then not only alive but enjoying holding court in Brighton. Elizabeth, on the other hand, was worn out, shuttling between attendance on Frank in Brighton and winding up the term in Stoke-on-Trent. With Frank on the mend, she felt able to accept the offer of a holiday in Venice with his sister Mary Pakenham and their mutual friend, David Cecil. Their host, the novelist Leslie (L. P.) Hartley, owned an apartment overlooking the water and a gondola, in which they explored the canals. There were also expeditions to Bologna and Ravenna and finally a few enjoyable days in Rome alone with Mary (who, incidentally, disliked her own name and was always known to Elizabeth as Maria).

In was Elizabeth's first visit to Italy and a magical time for them all. David was on the brink of his engagement to Rachel MacCarthy and as they floated down the canals he reflected his mood by reading to them Keats's romantic poem 'Eve of St Mark'. Mary, then twenty-two, was not only emotionally close to Frank but so like him in speech and manner as to give Elizabeth particular pleasure. Mary soon became a strong supporter of Elizabeth and the two became lifelong friends. They had much in common; Mary was a student at art school and had spent a term at boarding school with Armorel.

In April 1931 Frank returned to the Conservative research department and Elizabeth to her students. In May she spoke in support of the Labour candidate at the Gloucestershire by-election in Stroud. Frank's letters were no longer filled with recriminations, rather there were plans for them to return to Oxford together to dance again at the Balliol Commem. Ball at the end of the academic year. There, at last, in June 1931, they publicly announced their engagement. Yet even on that momentous evening Frank could not stay awake after midnight; Elizabeth found an undergraduate's empty bed in which they slept soundly and chastely until an outraged scout, coming upon them the next morning, inferred the worst and drove them out.

Once their decision was made, plans went smoothly, each winning the respect of the other's family. Lady Longford, Frank's mother, was already an invalid suffering severely from arthritis, forced by pain to withdraw from social life. She died two years later in 1933, but in that time Elizabeth established a good relationship with her mother-in-law. Mr Harman now approved of Frank, believing that the size of his head indicated a powerful brain! Frank's mother liked tall men and was therefore disposed to approve of Mr Harman, while 'her pleasure at her new daughter-in-law was unconcealed'.[7] Frank's grandmother, the Countess of Jersey, had liked and respected Elizabeth's great-uncle Joseph Chamberlain. In her day Lady Jersey had been an eminent political hostess and Joe Chamberlain had frequently attended her salons in the early years of the century. Elizabeth, with her gaiety and energy, was warmly welcomed by all of Frank's bright young friends, except for Evelyn Waugh, who falsely imputed his own snobbery to the Longfords. For many years he greeted Elizabeth with, 'How's the hockey?' – implying an immature interest in schoolgirl pursuits, a comment that never failed to rile her.

Elizabeth's social life in Stoke-on-Trent differed greatly from Frank's London world, in which he was on familiar terms with the Duchess of York (who became Queen Elizabeth in 1936), Nancy Astor and Charlie Chaplin. Frank's parties had earlier contributed to their prickly relations. 'I can't find fault in you,' Frank had written in February 1931, 'except your attitude to my attitude to the kind of parties I like. I think you are rather hard on me . . .' Sixty years later Elizabeth dismisses this as nothing more than a symptom of the general problems between them in the period before their official engagement. It is difficult not to speculate on the effect of Elizabeth's austere upbringing; someone who had been brought up to take her pleasures moderately might well feel uncomfortable with the exuberant young set whose company Frank so much enjoyed.

Frank and subsequently Elizabeth found no lasting problem in bridging the two worlds. In the summer of their engagement Frank visited Elizabeth at the Hobsons', who obligingly vacated their double bed for the couple. Believing it churlish to decline this generosity, they accepted the offer and slept with a bolster between them.

By this time Elizabeth had decided to abandon her studies in London, a decision for which Evan Durbin rather than Frank was responsible. Evan insisted, with all the authority of a newly appointed lecturer at the London School of Economics, that 'One second is bearable but two would mean that you were a second-class person' (*The Pebbled Shore*, p. 106). In July 1931 they went to East Sussex to visit Frank's great-aunt Caroline Pakenham at Bernhurst – the property destined for Frank, who was her acknowledged heir. Great-aunt Caroline was then eighty-nine and although she was to live for another seven years, her mind was beginning to wander. Greeting Frank as if he had just returned from a day with the Boy Scouts, she pointed at Elizabeth and asked, 'Who is that woman? I didn't invite her'. Dinner then became a contest in which both her butler and her long-suffering companion struggled to keep the old lady's false teeth in place. Some weeks later they were again invited to Pakenham, where there was a house full of guests including Elizabeth's sister. 'Kitty is a great success and seems to be enjoying the party very much . . .' Elizabeth wrote to her mother (from Ireland, 2nd September). 'As for me, the thought of being married next month is one over which I gloat in secret.'

Mrs Harman made herself responsible for all the wedding arrangements: no parsimony was to undermine what was to be a society wedding on 27th October at St Margaret's, Westminster, followed by a reception at Grosvenor House, Park

Lane. Mrs Harman could be formidable, but even she was unable to control the recently constituted national government, which called a general election for the same day. The wedding was consequently postponed to 3rd November.

Elizabeth decided to be a traditional bride in cream satin, making, according to old Lady Jersey, most effective use of the Longford Brussels lace veil. She was escorted by twelve bridesmaids, all sisters or cousins of the bride or bridegroom. Each bridesmaid wore a different-coloured velvet jacket over her white satin dress, thereby adding a blaze of colour to the bridal procession. Frank and his best man, Lord Birkenhead, went to Westminster Abbey by mistake – there was no one else there, and his best man assured Frank that 'people don't go to weddings much these days' (*The Pebbled Shore*, p. 133). By the time they realised that they should be next door in St Margaret's, they were late, but Elizabeth was later.

The traditional service, but without an address, was performed by Canon William Carnegie, a Chamberlain connection by marriage, and an eminent churchman and respected author of theological works.[8] Chamberlain and Harman relations turned out in force, but Frank's boss, Neville Chamberlain, neither came himself nor allowed anyone from the research department to go on from the church to the reception. It was thought that he was giving Frank a wide berth on account of rumours that he was about to become a socialist.

4

Settling in to Married Life

The night of 3rd November was exceptionally wild, making the stormy Irish Sea an unfortunate choice for a wedding night. The journey began badly with a mix-up over reservations on the mail train to Liverpool, and even from the luxury of a state cabin amidships Frank had to battle successfully against seasickness, with heavy seas prolonging their crossing by two hours. On account of the delay they lost the connection from Dun Laoghaire to Mullingar, where Edward's car, driven by Mr White, was waiting to take them to Connemara; Frank's brother had lent them both the car and his chauffeur for their honeymoon. Exhausted, they made for Pakenham, intending to take a day's rest before continuing the journey – this turned out to be yet another unfortunate choice. Their memories were of a house alive with laughter and song and people. Instead they found it vast, solitary and melancholy.

Years later Elizabeth was to impress upon her eldest daughter, Antonia, 'Never forget that, whatever they tell you, sex is extremely enjoyable.' But on that first night at Pakenham 'sex [was not] the elixir and panacea it was to become' (*The Pebbled Shore*, p. 136). Neither Lady Longford nor Mrs Harman had been able to broach the subject with the young couple and they had gone for instruction to a gynaecologist, Dr Helena Wright, MRCS, LRCP, medical officer of the Marie Stopes Memorial Clinic, whose advice was not, however, immediately helpful on their marriage night.

After one night at Pakenham, Frank and Elizabeth were driven to the west coast where they spent three 'perfect' days in a hotel in Connemara before motoring back to Meath to spend the rest of the week with Frank's Aunt Beatrice and her husband. Lord Dunsany was a writer and an eccentric and Lady Dunsany managed the castle with the minimum of staff. Elizabeth quickly sized up this situation and rescued the shoes that Frank had left in the corridor outside their door. 'But who's going to clean my shoes?' he demanded indignantly. 'I'll do them for you this once,' said she, 'but don't you go thinking that I'm going to clean your shoes for the rest of our married life.'

On the following day even this small task was beyond Elizabeth, for she had had the misfortune to be incapacitated by her monthly period. From the age of fourteen, periods had always been accompanied by severe pain, for which neither of her parents, both doctors, had proffered anything other than stoical acceptance. Elizabeth subsequently described what she went through at Dunsany as worse than the pains of childbirth. Alarmed by her distress, Aunt Beatrice summoned the doctor, who administered pain-killers and a sedative, but confirmed the straightforward diagnosis of dysmenorrhea (painful periods). Elizabeth asked if having a baby would cure the problem. The doctor thought that it might – an opinion that Elizabeth put to the test almost immediately.

Despite Elizabeth's indisposition it had been a wonderful week, which ended all too quickly as Elizabeth and Frank came back to their new home, Stairways, in the Buckinghamshire village of Stone. Stairways had been contrived from a pair of the Peverel estate workers' cottages knocked into one, and was made available to them by Frank's mother. She was then living a stone's throw away at Peverel Court, bought by the Longfords in 1911. Their new home, named for the staircase at either end of it, was habitable, but the redecorating was still under way and the young couple scratched the date and their initials on the plaster of the chimney breasts in two of the upstairs rooms. (These were still there sixty-five years later when the bedroom walls were stripped down for repapering.) Compared with the Victorian Peverel Court, Stairways was small and cramped, with low cottage ceilings, but nonetheless there was space for four guests in addition to Mr and Mrs Morris, the couple who acted as chauffeur/houseman and cook/parlour maid. The garden, behind an unkempt privet hedge, was meagre and unremarkable apart from one prolific damson tree.

Many newly-weds might be alarmed to have a mother-in-law living on their doorstep, but Elizabeth was delighted. Although she never became intimate with Lady Longford, each respected the other, and Elizabeth believed that it was the struggle with arthritis that made her mother-in-law so distant. Mary Longford was fifty-one at this time, but already so disabled that she could only manage to get about in her baby Austin; the concrete paths she laid down in order to be able to move around the estate in her car are still in place. Violet and Julia, the two youngest Pakenham girls, were unmarried, living at home, and were constantly in and out of Stairways. Violet in particular enjoyed replanning the garden with Elizabeth, although both were more enthusiastic than knowledgable. On one occasion while attempting to tidy the privet hedge they managed to cut off the telephone by severing the wires. Violet recalls nights that were so hot that they slept on the gravel outside the front door, to be awoken by the arrival of the gardener with his squeaking boots.[1] Frank's mother had been an enthusiastic gardener and was happy to offer advice on the purchase of shrubs and plants, which, together with grass seed and manure, formed a considerable item in the Pakenhams' first account book (which incidentally is still extant).

The house was constantly full of friends. John Betjeman came to stay with Penelope Chetwode, who was later to become his wife. Penelope had been known to Frank: he had been at Eton with her brother Roger. Penelope's marriage to John Betjeman contributed to Elizabeth's growing reputation as a matchmaker. Other frequent visitors were Esmond Warner, also an old Etonian, Naomi Mitchison, Hugh Gaitskell, Evan Durbin, Evelyn Waugh and Frank's uncle Eddie Dunsany.[2] They played bridge or embarrassing games of self-revelation. They talked and argued endlessly as they huddled round the smoking fire or lounged in the garden. Often Frank and Elizabeth were away themselves staying at Cliveden, Hatfield or Clandeboye, so different from their own more modest, yet comfortable cottage.

In February 1932, a month or two after she had settled at Stairways, Elizabeth again visited Dr Helena Wright, who confirmed that she was pregnant. Following her normal practice, the doctor inserted a stiff, rubber-like contraption, explaining that this was necessary to keep the foetus in the right position and to prevent miscarriage. She also insisted on a strict dietary regime: plenty of lettuce and egg white, and no fruit, alcohol or cigarettes. Despite Dr Wright's somewhat abrupt manner Elizabeth had great faith in her. She consulted her over all her pregnancies and followed her advice on the determination of the sexes. Dr Wright took the view that male sperm preferred an alkaline solution, female sperm an acid solution. By taking the appropriate douche half an hour before intercourse she maintained that it was possible to ensure the desired sex.

Elizabeth's first pregnancy was her worst; she felt sick and wretched for most of the time and the smell of distemper at Stairways did little to improve matters. Frank was still working at the research department in London, commuting by train from Princes Risborough. Although Bill Morris drove him the eight or so miles to the station and met him in the evening Bill usually lost his way. Elizabeth had never before been kept waiting for dinner, and by the time Frank arrived home, sometimes having missed his train, she was often in floods of tears, convinced that he had been involved in an accident or even that he had decided not to come home at all. Frank knew little of women, nothing about the mood swings of pregnancy and nothing about how to deal with a fractious wife.

Frank and Elizabeth had argued vociferously before their marriage and these arguments continued afterwards. The only subject that was never in contention was Elizabeth's determination to live a full life, by which she meant one that embraced both family and career. In this Frank has given unstinting support and encouragement and has always taken great pride in her achievements. There was therefore never any question of Elizabeth's ceasing to work with the WEA in Staffordshire or withdrawing from her commitment to the Labour Party. Despite morning sickness she continued to lecture in Stoke-on-Trent during her first pregnancy, spending one or two nights in London on the way in a rented room on the Embankment that was small, shabby and at constant risk from flooding.

Elizabeth's determination to go on working was unusual for a woman in her position. Her own mother, who had broken with convention in the choice of her medical career, had not continued in practice after her marriage. As her pregnancy advanced Elizabeth had to reduce the number of lectures, but her presentation at Court, arranged for May 1932, could not easily be put off. She had agreed to this at the request of her mother-in-law, who had made it plain on their return from honeymoon that this was expected. Elizabeth, who had not been presented before, raised no objection apart from a concern about being pregnant.[3]

Lady Longford swept Elizabeth's hesitation aside, assuring her that 'the first one never shows'. In May Elizabeth received a command to attend Court to be presented to King George V and Queen Mary by her aunt Helen Chamberlain, together with her cousin Drusilla Hyndson, née Chamberlain (daughter of John Chamberlain, Arthur Chamberlain's youngest son).

The nonconformist Chamberlains had, for the most part, held themselves aloof from the Establishment. Now Elizabeth found herself following precise, formal Court protocol. As instructed, she was dressed in a white evening gown and long white gloves with an ostrich feather in her hair. On such occasions the wait outside the palace was notorious for its tedium: all the guests were under strict instructions regarding time of arrival, but they tended to arrive simultaneously early. There was nothing for it but to drive endlessly round and round Queen Victoria's statue, while a queue of cars stretched back up The Mall. There the crowds enjoyed themselves gawping at the royal guests inside their cars. Elizabeth, forewarned of the likely delay, brought a game of backgammon with her; the following morning a newspaper carried a photograph of herself and Drusilla sitting in the car in their finery, with the backgammon board between them. Once inside the palace there was more waiting before they finally reached the throne room, where King George V and Queen Mary awaited their curtsey. This was no quick bob but a deep obeisance, requiring skill and practice; quite often dressmakers combined a rehearsal of the curtsey with a fitting for the dress. Elizabeth, with the added encumbrance of pregnancy, had practised conscientiously, but in her eagerness to get a good look at the King and Queen, sank too low, was unable to get up again and had to be rescued by a Lord-in-Waiting.

Little more than three months later, in the early hours of 27th August 1932, Antonia Margaret Caroline Pakenham was born at 48 Sussex Gardens, weighing eight pounds four ounces. The house had been lent for the birth by Frank's Aunt Cynthia Slessor.[4] The nine-hour labour had not been easy; the baby, at first in no hurry, finally arrived at such speed that there was no time to give chloroform. Elizabeth was left battered and requiring several stitches. Dr Maud Chadburn, the Harley Street gynaecologist who supervised the birth, had been recommended by Henry Lamb, who was married to Frank's sister Pansy.[5] Dr Chadburn was radical in her approach, and, unusually for the time, raised no objection to Frank's presence throughout. She insisted that her patients remain on their backs during labour, which was then a new idea and one that Elizabeth found increased her discomfort. Elizabeth decided that in future she would be delivered by her own GP in her own home and in her own bed.

The name Antonia was chosen from Willa Cather's novel *My Antonia*, but Frank's sister Maria, the first visitor, noticing the baby's jaundiced skin, nicknamed her 'Mrs Gandhi'! Mr Harman came to admire his first grandchild and was blatantly disappointed by her sex. 'A man needs a son,' he told Elizabeth. 'But I was your first child,' she protested. Flowers poured in, visitors brought yet more tributes and the only long face in Sussex Gardens was on Miss Effie Rendell, the monthly nurse, who was put out at having to find so many vases. She was also incensed by Desmond Ryan, an old Oxford friend, who turned up with peaches in brandy. 'Baby simply hates alcohol' (*The Pebbled Shore*, p. 143).

They returned to Stairways as soon as Elizabeth was fit to do so and in September were on their way to visit several friends in Ireland, taking the baby and her nurse with them. Travel is one of the few issues on which Frank and Elizabeth hold opposing views. Elizabeth loves to go away and Frank hates it, but fortunately he never thinks of travelling to Ireland as anything other than going home. Frank's enthusiasm for Ireland is shared by Elizabeth, partly because from her nursery days she has always been biased in favour of anyone whom she perceives to be disadvantaged. Moreover, 'Ireland was the only political problem – or rather political answer – on which I accepted without question the judgement of Frank's heart and head,' Elizabeth wrote in her memoirs (*The Pebbled Shore*, p. 146). In view of the political disagreements of their engagement this was a surprising admission.

During this Irish holiday their first visit was to Lord and

Lady Dufferin and Ava at Clandeboye, near Belfast. Basil and Maureen Dufferin were old friends; Frank had been best man at their wedding, and Elizabeth was about to invite Maureen to be one of Antonia's godmothers. All Elizabeth's babies became used to travel from the earliest age. She breastfed them for at least six months, but this in no way restricted her activities. Most of her friends lived in large houses, and at Clandeboye Antonia and her nurse shared the nursery with the Dufferins' one-year-old daughter, Caroline. From Clandeboye they went south to Pakenham and from there to county Wicklow to stay with Frank's friend Bob Barton in Glendalough. It was during this visit to Ireland that Frank was asked to write the history of the 1921 Irish Partition Treaty. *Peace by Ordeal* was published to acclaim in 1935, was quickly recognised as a standard work and has been reprinted three times, most recently in 1992.

Returning to Stairways in October after the Irish holiday, Elizabeth engaged Nancy, a robust girl from Devon, to take charge of Antonia, who was shortly to be christened. Breaking with Unitarian teaching and despite the fact that she herself had not been christened, Elizabeth had her first six children baptised into the Anglican Church. They were also generously endowed with godparents, many of Antonia's being close relatives. Mary Pakenham and Edward Longford, Frank's sister and brother, his brother-in-law Henry Lamb, his uncle Arthur Villiers and Elizabeth's sister Kitty all stood as godparents, together with two close friends, Margaret Birkenhead, widow of the first Earl of Birkenhead, and Maureen Dufferin and Ava. For Elizabeth, in contrast to Frank, the principal significance of the ceremony was social rather than religious, and presumably it was a similar sentiment that brought Mrs Harman to the local church in Stone to be present at the christening of her first grandchild.

Not long after Antonia's christening, Elizabeth again became pregnant and did not therefore return to Stoke-on-Trent as a regular WEA lecturer, although she continued to be called upon occasionally by the WEA. She had also been taken on by Oxford to give University extension lectures on literature, economics or contemporary politics in different locations. She was now an experienced and talented speaker and enjoyed the work, although she preferred her WEA students to those attending the extension lectures, most of whom were merely adding a gloss to an already adequate education. The thirst and need of the WEA students was so much greater.

In 1934 Elizabeth gave a series of University extension lectures at Canterbury in which she compared Victorian and Edwardian writers with those of the present day, dwelling at some length on Joseph Conrad's *Arrow of Gold*. Her audience consisted largely of white-collar workers and clergy wives. She was somewhat disconcerted afterwards to discover that among the ladies sitting in the front row enjoying her discourse was Joseph Conrad's widow.

Thomas was born on 14th August 1933 and caused some anxiety in the nursery. The baby arrived a few days before Antonia's first birthday and she gave him a very uncertain welcome; fortunately Elizabeth happened to hear the baby's muffled cries on the day that Antonia filled his cot with toys to the point of suffocation (whether from spite or affection Elizabeth never discovered). Elizabeth placed full trust in Nancy, her nanny, although a friend, Anne Martelli, thought that the girl was too harsh with the children and told Elizabeth that Nancy sometimes put Thomas under the cold tap to keep him quiet. Elizabeth had never seen Nancy do any such thing and dismissed the idea out of hand.

All the Pakenham children were boisterous. According to one story, apparently apocryphal (no direct source is discoverable) but frequently repeated among the family, Elizabeth was told that one of the nannies gave the children a whiff of gas when they got out of hand. In her anxiety she uncharacteristically consulted Frank, who could offer no solution. 'We will just have to watch and pray,' said Elizabeth. 'Yes,' said

Frank. 'You watch, I'll pray.' Elizabeth herself could be quite hard on the children. To this day Thomas shudders to recall a summer holiday with the Martellis at Brancaster, in Norfolk, when he was two and his mother carried him screaming into the freezing sea.

In 1933, two years after her marriage, life was becoming more secure for Elizabeth, with a good possibility that Frank would obtain a full-time post as a lecturer in politics at Christ Church, which would double his salary to £1000. Frank's job in the Conservative research department had been affected by Neville Chamberlain's departure to become Chancellor of the Exchequer in 1931; after Neville had left, the department did little work of significance. Frank resigned in 1932, and after an unsuccessful attempt to become a journalist on the *Daily Mail* was given a part-time lectureship in 1932 at the London School of Economics, combining this with research for *Peace by Ordeal*. Elizabeth was learning to drive and had grasped the basics after half a dozen lessons (the driving test was not introduced until March 1935). She therefore had no hesitation in setting out on the eighteen-mile journey to Oxford. Driving the car smartly out of the gate on to the dangerous road, she saw a vehicle approaching, slammed her foot down, missed the brake, hit the accelerator and sent the car straight into the ditch opposite. Fortunately she was unhurt and in no way put off by this disastrous beginning. Frank never learnt to drive, relying on Elizabeth until reluctantly she had to surrender her licence at eighty-eight, when glaucoma was diagnosed.

In the summer of 1934 she and Frank were invited to attend a peace conference at Bouffémont on the outskirts of Paris. Here Elizabeth had a narrow escape caused by a recurrence of her childhood habit of sleep-walking. She awoke to find herself on the balcony of their bedroom, about to step into what she believed to be an enticing moonlit garden but which was in fact a concrete yard thirty feet below. The following night Frank placed his bed across the window, only to be awoken by

Elizabeth attempting to clamber over him. On the third night they locked all the doors. This was, for whatever reason, the last occurrence of her sleep-walking.

A few months earlier Frank's lectureship at Christ Church had been confirmed, convincing Elizabeth that a house in Oxford had become a necessity. Stairways was isolated and with the death of Lady Longford in 1933 and the consequent sale of Peverel Court (Stairways not being included in the sale), Elizabeth had lost the companionable visits of her sisters-in-law, Violet and Julia. In the summer of 1934 she and Frank moved to a rented, modern, stone house called Singletree, between the village of Iffley and the rapidly expanding industrial suburb of Cowley. Singletree was on the outskirts of the city – there were neither shops nor schools close by and the development of a new estate, which was effectively to block the view of the city, was only months away. Yet the house had advantages: it was light and spacious – Antonia, now an energetic two-year-old, revelled in her large new nursery – and the Labour movement in Cowley was exceedingly active.

Elizabeth was becoming increasingly involved with politics. She joined the local branch of the Labour Party in Cowley, and Singletree became a regular venue for the Party's meetings; she took part in all the fund-raising events, outings and socials, especially those that involved the wives. She felt herself to be fully identified with the Cowley 'Labour women'. In the spring of 1935 she was invited to Cambridge by an Irish undergraduate, Richard Llewellyn-Davies, of King's College. (His mother, Moya, was a friend of Frank's who had helped him with his work on *Peace by Ordeal.*) Richard and a group of friends, among whom were a number of communists, were organising a reception party to welcome a band of hunger marchers on their way south to London. Throughout the 1930s, bands of unemployed workers from the depressed industrial centres converged on London where they held protests in Downing Street. The Jarrow March of 1936 was the most famous. They made little impact in London, but aroused sympathy and were an effective propaganda weapon.

Elizabeth was delighted to have this opportunity; grasping a banner and chanting slogans, she joined the students as they marched to the meeting-point on the outskirts of the town. 'Scholarships not battleships,' they barracked, breaking into a jingle when the comrades began to straggle:

> One two three four
> What are we for?
> We're for the working class
> Down with the ruling class! (*The Pebbled Shore*, p. 160).

Perhaps it was Elizabeth's association with the marchers that persuaded the Cheltenham Labour Party to consider her for selection as their candidate in the anticipated general election. Cheltenham, home of 'lost Colonels' (*The Pebbled Shore*, p. 161) was most unlikely to return a socialist to Westminster. In the 1931 election the Conservatives achieved a record majority of 17,000; Labour, which had contested the seat only three times, had never managed to poll more than 5,263 votes. Elizabeth was well aware of the odds, but she did not hesitate to accept the challenge. Frank, having wavered in his loyalty to the Conservative Party for some time, finally severed all official links by resigning from that Conservative stronghold, the Carlton Club. Twelve months later he became a member of the Labour Party.

In her campaign Elizabeth, adhering closely to official Labour policy, advocated support for the League of Nations, the admission of Russia to the League and opposition to rearmament. She did not doubt the menace of Hitler's growing ambitions, but like so many she believed that both Hitler and Mussolini could be contained by the collective security of an armed European alliance that would obviate the need for rearmament. She canvassed enthusiastically for nationalisation, stressing particularly railways and banks – the local industries that would be directly affected. She had significant support; as well as Frank, Dick Crossman, Naomi Mitchison, Aidan Crawley (later to be both a Labour and a Conservative MP), the economist Roy Harrod and the historian Max Beloff all spoke at her meetings. *Isis* was also behind her, reporting (13th November 1935) that 'packed meetings have approved her energy and enthusiasm.' Elizabeth's genuine love for people made her a great success on the doorstep. 'The draughtier the alleyway, the happier I was. I just enjoyed the conversations and as a result did six people in an hour instead of twenty' (interview with Brian Connell in *The Times*, 1976).

On the eve of the poll she received messages of support from her mother, Uncle Eddie Dunsany and WEA friends from Stoke-on-Trent. Inevitably the Labour Party lost, but although the Conservative candidate, Sir Walter Preston, polled 18,574 to her 7,784, she had gained an increase of over two and a half thousand Labour votes, noticeably reducing his previous majority. At the end of the contest a Labour Party dinner was held at the Cadena Corner Café in Cheltenham, where Elizabeth was applauded for her 'youth, energy, brains and above all for her personality' (*Cheltenham Echo*, November 1935). Stafford Cripps, the future Labour Chancellor of the Exchequer, also sent a personal note of congratulation.[6]

Two days before the poll Frank wrote to Elizabeth at Charlton Kings where she had been lodging with an ex-suffragette. He was longing to have her back, but also told her of his concern lest she experience a sense of anti-climax when the contest was over. He should have known better. Elizabeth plunged straight back into University extension lectures, concentrating on 'Makers of the Modern World', 'Europe Today' and similar contemporary issues. Then in May 1936 Frank was injured at a meeting organised in Oxford by Oswald Mosley and his British Union of Fascists, which had ended in a free-for-all between the Mosleyites and the socialists. Frank was concussed and kicked in the kidneys by the jackbooted blackshirts, and Elizabeth temporarily dropped her other commitments in order to care for him. At the time neither of them realised that she was about to be asked to take on a new commitment that would demand consistent absence from home.

5

A Full Life

In the summer of 1936 Elizabeth was on holiday at the seaside with Antonia and Thomas when she received a letter from the Labour agent for the King's Norton division of Birmingham. Tom Baxter expressed the hope that she would allow her name to go before the selection committee who were looking for a prospective Labour candidate.

King's Norton was a markedly different constituency from Cheltenham, for the local Bournville chocolate factory and the Austin car works ensured a strong body of potential Labour voters. The sitting MP was the Conservative Ronald Cartland (brother of the novelist Barbara Cartland), but the prospects for Labour were sufficiently good to attract strong candidates. Elizabeth's rivals were Anthony Greenwood, the son of the Labour leader, Arthur Greenwood, and Leonard Woolf (husband of the writer Virginia), a former civil servant and an expert on the Far East and colonialism. Both were formidable opponents.

Frank was delighted at the possibility that Elizabeth might nurse the King's Norton constituency and had every confidence that she could win the seat. Radical Joe – her great-uncle Joseph Chamberlain – had not been forgotten in Birmingham and as far as the selection committee was concerned the relationship was clearly an advantage, as was her sex. Ronald Cartland's good looks were so striking that there was a view that he should be opposed by a young and attractive woman; Elizabeth's speech to the committee was as striking as her appearance and she was selected. Shortly before this she had become aware she was pregnant with her third child. She and Frank were staying with the Duke and Duchess of Devonshire at Compton Place, near Eastbourne, and while playing bridge she realised that she was going to be sick. She got as far as the hall, where she had no option but to seize a silver salver. With some apprehension she told Tom Baxter that she was expecting another child. Having recently become a father himself, Tom was not unduly concerned and was even confident that the mother of three young children would have a particular appeal to women voters at the next general election.

In September 1936 Elizabeth and Frank were invited to Berlin for a conference on democracy and peace with fellow European academics. Three years of Hitler's rule had already caused sufficient alarm to prompt serious doubts about the wisdom of going to Berlin at all. They decided in favour of the trip, but took with them an identifiably left-wing publication, which they left open in their hotel room, a hair carefully placed across it. If they were under surveillance their room would be searched and the hair displaced. They detected no sign of this and the weekend passed uneventfully, neither the Pakenhams nor the German professors being moved to adjust their respective positions. On their return Frank finally became a member of the Labour Party, joining the Cowley and Iffley branch to which Elizabeth had belonged for two years. At last they were a political team.

With interesting work, a third child on the way and the back-up of an efficient household, Elizabeth was increasingly satisfied with her full life. She was a good organiser, so although political commitments meant that she had to be away at weekends as well as during the week, the household ran smoothly. First thing on a Monday morning she discussed the coming week with her new nanny, twenty-year-old Jean Birch, who had replaced Nancy when she left to get married. Jean worked hard and rarely had time off at the weekend, but has warm and affectionate memories of her five years with the Pakenhams. She especially enjoyed those evenings when both Frank and the cook were out and she and Elizabeth would sit for hours at the kitchen table, talking non-stop over their poached eggs – neither being capable of producing anything more ambitious.

Christmas celebrations in Birmingham at the end of 1936, on top of her regular meetings, made serious inroads into Elizabeth's time. Fortunately her mother's sister, Aunt Bertha Hope, came to the rescue with an offer of accommodation in Birmingham. On 11th December 1936 Elizabeth listened to the abdication broadcast of Edward VIII in the Hopes' drawing room. She described her feelings in *The Pebbled Shore*: 'Could this really be the King speaking? To me it sounded more like the hero of a "penny dreadful" with his uninhibited clichés about "the woman I love". All my Chamberlain blood repudiated this sin against the dignity of office' (p. 177).

They had planned to spend Christmas with Frank's eldest sister, Pansy, and her husband, Henry Lamb, at Coombe Bissett, in Wiltshire. In the event Thomas developed a feverish sore throat. Elizabeth and Frank therefore took Antonia to the Lambs, as planned, but left Thomas in Oxford with Jean. A day or two later he was unable to lift his arm or turn his head and the doctor called in a second opinion. Elizabeth hastily returned. Thomas was rushed to the Wingfield Hospital in Headington where it was confirmed that he was suffering from the dreaded infantile paralysis or polio (a terrible scourge until the discovery in 1955 of an effective vaccine by Dr Jonas Salk and the later universal availability of an oral vaccine developed by Albert Sabin, which more or less eliminated the disease).

Thomas, then aged three and a half, can still recall the anguish of being plucked from his bed in the middle of the night, and the ensuing misery of the months in hospital. Although he received daily visits from Elizabeth and Frank, and from Antonia who was brought to the hospital by his adored nanny, Jean, he felt that his mother abandoned him in his need. During this period he developed a stammer. After three months, on 8th April 1937, wearing a neck brace and with his arm supported by a splint, Thomas was brought home. The source of the disease was never traced. Some said that he must have contracted polio at the Christmas party given by the Cowley Labour Club, a charge Elizabeth indignantly denies. Whatever the case, Thomas recovered fully, but like many polio victims has developed some muscular weakness in later years.

The third baby was expected in April and Elizabeth again planned a home delivery with the support of Sammy, as the monthly nurse was affectionately known. Nurse Samways's time seemed to be taken up in delivering Chamberlain babies and she became a well-loved family institution. Like Antonia, Paddy arrived at great speed and preceded the arrival of the doctor. Sammy, fully occupied with Elizabeth, summoned Frank to open the sealed drum containing the sterilised dressings. Elizabeth, knowing that Frank could not be trusted with handling a sharp instrument, shouted instructions from her bed. As usual Elizabeth breastfed her baby. When she drove to Birmingham on her regular visits to her constituents, Paddy travelled in the back of the car in his moses basket. Jean, now responsible for three young children, was given both a salary increase and additional time off.

In working out their income, Frank and Elizabeth had not taken into account the demands that would be made by a growing family, and their economic situation was becoming increasingly straitened. Fortunately when Paddy was four months old their long-term prospects began to improve. When the new baby was taken to visit Great-Aunt Caroline at Bernhurst, Frank's Uncle Bingo – Major Edward Pakenham – was sufficiently impressed to change his will in favour of Frank and his growing family, rather than leaving everything to

Edward, the older brother. (Edward by this time was out of family favour because of his perceived overgenerosity to the Gate Theatre.) The future was encouraging, with Uncle Bingo's inheritance and the prospect that Bernhurst would be left to them by Great-Aunt Caroline. Nevertheless, their current financial situation caused Elizabeth some concern. From time to time she would order an economy drive, insisting on either jam or cake for nursery tea, but not both. The children would grumble and Jean would tell them to be patient: sure enough, by the end of the week things would have quietly reverted to normal. When Paddy had outgrown his second-hand pram, Elizabeth tried to exchange it for a push-chair and was most indignant to be offered only five shillings (25p) for the wheels, the rest of the pram being considered worthless!

Although she was careful Elizabeth could also be generous. She insisted on paying the cost of Jean's dental treatment and, after a year or so at Singletree, the Pakenhams had become a regular port of call for gentlemen of the road. They looked on Elizabeth as a soft touch, although when she offered Frank's overcoat to one tramp he refused to accept it, much less wear it.

On the days when Jean was off duty, Elizabeth generally looked after the children herself. There was no doubt of her affection, but she was exceedingly busy and could be impatient. Shouting matches were not unknown; indeed, Rachel, the fifth child, who was born five years after Paddy, is convinced that her mother developed strong lungs – an essential for public speaking before the regular use of microphones – as a result of yelling at them all. Jean remembers telling Thomas that he must refer a particular question to his mother rather than herself. 'But Jean,' he replied, 'you are not nearly so fierce as Mummy.' Jean's day off could also spark a row between Frank and Elizabeth. When Frank came home from Christ Church he liked to have the children around him, but Elizabeth had been looking after them all day and wanted to have Frank to herself. After one such altercation she lost her temper and hurled a telephone directory at him, shouting, 'If that's how you feel you can put them to bed yourself.'

Given the pressures under which she was living, Elizabeth's short temper is less than surprising. Frank's commitments were also increasing, which inevitably affected her. In November 1937 he had won a seat on the Oxford city council during a by-election for the Cowley and Iffley ward. Elizabeth, increasingly absorbed by activities for her King's Norton constituency, was however attracting somewhat unfavourable notice from the Labour leadership. She had joined the Socialist League, founded by the Labour politician Stafford Cripps, which largely drew its membership from the left wing of the Labour Party and advocated the inclusion of communists in the party, to which both the Labour Party and the trade union movement were adamantly opposed, having already experienced the insidious results of communist infiltration. Supporters and members of the Socialist League were openly contemptuous, referring to the Labour leadership as 'reactionary old buffers' (*The Pebbled Shore*, p. 182) and the League was expelled from the party in 1936, to be followed in 1938 by Cripps himself. Elizabeth left the League in 1938, but did not withdraw her support from Cripps; she could not forget how he had gone out of his way to support her when she had been fighting the Cheltenham seat in 1935.

In Birmingham Elizabeth was gaining a reputation for hard work and effective public speaking, and her support for the Socialist League attracted little or no criticism. Her Chamberlain connection was advantageous in Labour eyes, even though her cousin Neville Chamberlain had replaced Stanley Baldwin as leader of the Conservative Party and Prime Minister in 1937. Neville was her mother's favourite cousin and had indeed wished to marry Katherine Chamberlain before Nat Harman came into her life. Elizabeth had always felt guilty about her opposition to Neville, but never sufficiently so to consider changing her allegiance. Hugh Dalton, Chairman of the National Executive Committee of the Labour Party and future Chancellor of the Exchequer in the Attlee government, was an ardent opponent of Chamberlain's policy of appeasement in the years preceding the Second World War. He invited Elizabeth to speak in Birmingham Town Hall on collective security, which was perceived by a large section of the Labour Party as the appropriate response to Hitler. The Town Hall was packed and, although very well prepared, she was physically sick with nerves. 'What sort of government is this,' she demanded, 'that cannot say boo to the goose-step?' (*The Pebbled Shore*, p. 185).

Despite her nerves the speech was a great success and the forerunner of various interventions that she would make at future Labour Party conferences. When she spoke at the conference in 1937, Ernest Bevin,[1] the future Foreign Secretary in Attlee's government, suggested that she should stand for the National Executive, although the suggestion was never followed up. On this occasion Elizabeth had the opportunity to meet Beatrice Webb. At the end of the conference, she had returned to her hotel and was busy packing when the manager appeared accompanied by an angry guest who claimed that she had booked the room from 12 noon and it was now hers. Elizabeth ostentatiously consulted her watch and insisted that the time was 11.55: in five minutes she would vacate the room, but not a moment sooner. Neither formidable lady was going to back down, so the manager tried a different tack. 'This is the Honourable Mrs Frank Pakenham,' said he, 'and this, Mrs Beatrice Webb.'[2] Pleasure swiftly replaced anger. Elizabeth and Beatrice knew each other well by reputation and were delighted at the unexpected meeting, each insisting that of course the other must have the room.

In the summer of 1938 Birmingham staged an ambitious historical pageant in celebration of the city's centenary of incorporation as a borough; Elizabeth was offered the main part of Eleanor of Aquitaine and Eleanor's consort, King Henry II, was played by her cousin, Michael Hope. Everything was taken very seriously, with numerous rehearsals and correct historical dress. Unfortunately for Elizabeth the eight-foot-wide, thirty-foot-long train attached to her shoulders produced severe neck-ache, but she persevered with her usual enthusiasm. The pageant, planned to last for a week, was extended to a fortnight by popular demand.

Elizabeth also featured in the *Oxford Mail,* which applauded her presence of mind in averting potential tragedy. She was taking part in a British Workers' Sports Association tennis rally at Boars Hill, and was changing courts at the end of a set when she heard a splash coming from the lily pond. Spotting a child's jersey, she quickly rescued the three-year-old. OXFORD COUNCILLOR'S WIFE'S PLUCK proclaimed the sexist headline.

Such parochial pageants and sports were taking place against the backdrop of an increasingly threatening European situation caused by Hitler's plans for German domination.[3] The conference held at Munich on 29th September 1938 was Chamberlain's third meeting with Hitler in as many weeks. He returned home sincerely believing that Hitler would honour the assurances that had been given and that war had been averted.[4] His optimism was shared by some, but many, including Frank and Elizabeth, were less sanguine.

1938 was a year of foreboding on the international scene, although for Frank and Elizabeth it brought increased financial security. Uncle Bingo died on 27th December 1937 and Great-Aunt Caroline in May 1938 at the age of 96. Neither death was a cause of great personal grief, for Frank had not been very close to either, but the double inheritance was to turn the Pakenhams into capitalists. They had never owned property. Their first home, Stairways, had been lent to them and Singletree, their Oxford house, was rented. They now found themselves the owners of property in London and in Sussex.

Uncle Bingo left a house in Norfolk Street, off Park Lane, and Aunt Caroline's estate in East Sussex included a furnished Georgian house with Regency additions and a five-acre garden. This eventually was to become an ideal family home. Great-Aunt Caroline's housekeeper, Mrs Pope, stayed on at Bernhurst and later joined the Pakenham household in Oxford where 'Popey' became an adored 'Granny' for the children and a constant support to Elizabeth.

It is something of a paradox that from the earliest awakening of Elizabeth's socialist conscience in 1931 when she became a WEA lecturer and lived with the Hobsons in Meir, she found herself moving with ease between the contrasting worlds of industrial, working-class Stoke-on-Trent and the wealthy comfort of Cliveden or Hatfield. Her criticism of the parties Frank enjoyed in the early 1930s had been provoked by the tension of their on/off engagement, and not by an objection on principle. She has always been pragmatic in her approach to aristocratic and wealthy friends whose political opinions differ very widely from her own. In her memoirs she makes no secret of the lack of congruence between practice and theory. 'Social principle,' she has asserted, 'did not require one to diminish the quality of life by giving up one's old friends' (*The Pebbled Shore*, p. 186). This of course meant staying in their houses, sharing, for limited periods at least, their lifestyle and gaining great pleasure from so doing. Later, when the children had reached the age of secondary schooling, the dilemma posed by the cost of principle was to cause more serious and heart-searching debate and to arouse criticism.

If temporary excursions into the world of capitalists were one thing, it was quite another to find oneself joining their ranks, and Elizabeth admits that she and Frank felt uncomfortable about their double windfall from Uncle Bingo and from Great-Aunt Caroline. They decided to 'fight all the harder with our new weapons to bring about peace and a less inequitable distribution of wealth' (*The Pebbled Shore*, p. 187),

71

but their ambivalent feelings perhaps explains why much of that inheritance was consumed by unsound schemes. A considerable sum was spent on the purchase of the *Town Crier*, a Birmingham local Labour weekly with a circulation of 2,600. Philip Toynbee, Frank's former pupil and a member of the communist party, was installed as editor; Pansy Lamb, Frank's sister, and Dick Crossman were recruited as regular contributors. Aunt Caroline's car was put at the disposal of the new circulation manager, George Tyler. Protest meetings were organised through the paper in order to enable its readers to lambast the government. It was hoped that the *Town Crier* would galvanise opposition to the government and lead to a Labour swing in Birmingham, taking both Elizabeth and Frank to Westminster. It did no such thing. Circulation fell drastically and the paper became a serious financial liability. After only five months it was sold at a considerable loss.

Their second attempt to make inherited wealth work for the cause was hardly more effective. During these post-Munich months of 1938–9 the question 'will there be war?' had become 'when will it start?' Urged on by the government, many families were organising shelters in their back gardens. Frank hired a gang of unemployed men from Cowley to dig trenches in the open space near the Pakenhams' house in Oxford as a defence in the event of enemy invasion. Wages were paid out of the recent legacies, but since there was no invasion the trenches were never used. This was just as well. When the city engineer examined them he discovered that much of the work had been poorly executed. Worldly possessions have never loomed large on the Pakenham list of priorities and the cash that for a brief time had created unquiet consciences was largely dwindling away.

It was another matter, however, when it came to political achievement, which has always been of supreme importance. For a brief period in 1938 there had seemed to be a real possibility that Elizabeth and Frank would enter Parliament together. Frank had been adopted as a prospective candidate for West Birmingham in 1938, two years after Elizabeth had been adopted for King's Norton. But no sooner had he accepted the West Birmingham offer than he was given the chance of standing for Oxford City. Frank knew and loved Oxford and was already known for his work on the Oxford council, where he had been popular and effective. The Labour leadership agreed to the transfer and Elizabeth was ecstatic (*The Pebbled Shore*, p. 189), imagining her triumphant arrival with Frank at the Palace of Westminster.

This prospect encouraged her to redouble her efforts in her own constituency, where she spent her days with her agent, Harold Nash, who lived on the Bournville estate with his wife, Elsie, and their two young sons, Norman and Sidney. Elizabeth grew fond of the two boys and invited them to spend a week at Singletree. The large house and unfamiliar food, however, made them miserably homesick and the visit was not a success.

In the spring of 1939 Elizabeth decided that, rather than rely on the Nash family, she needed her own base in Birmingham. She rented a small house in Mary Vale Road and there installed Mr White and his wife. White was the former chauffeur of Frank's brother Edward and he had driven Elizabeth and Frank on their honeymoon in Ireland. He was originally from Birmingham and delighted to come back. The Whites kept house for Elizabeth when she came to work in her constituency and acted as caretakers in her absence.

Shortly after moving in to Mary Vale Road, she brought Antonia and Thomas to stay for a week. Aged six and five, they were being taught by a friend's governess and were not yet going to school. For the week in Birmingham, however, Elizabeth decided to send them to the King's Norton Junior School on the Bournville estate. The experience was as much of a culture shock for Antonia and Thomas as Singletree had been for the Nash children. To make matters worse, Elizabeth forgot that the two would need to take money for their dinners and for mid-morning milk. Thus on the first day hunger was added to the bewilderment of being plunged into a very different environment with a crowd of strange children. The children were convinced that their mother was mad: neither Thomas nor Antonia has forgotten the incident.

The next significant change for Elizabeth came when Frank made the decision to join the territorials. He was conscious not only of the example of his father, killed at Gallipoli while manifesting outstanding courage, but also of Uncle Bingo's distinguished record in the First World War. In April 1939 Chamberlain's government had introduced limited conscription for twenty-year-old males. This was the first compulsory peacetime military service in modern times. It continued until 1960, when the last National Serviceman was called up. Seizing the opportunity to attempt to emulate his father, Frank volunteered as a Private in the Oxford and Buckinghamshire Light Infantry Territorials, while Elizabeth went for a brief holiday with her friend Naomi Mitchison in Argyll.

On her return Elizabeth began to make preparations for moving house again. Throughout the summer of 1939 billeting officers had been making arrangements for evacuation, assessing unused rooms that could provide accommodation in areas that were thought to be safe. Elizabeth knew that Single-tree would be totally unsuitable for the family as a wartime home. Close enough to the centre of Oxford to be in danger of air raids, it was remote from such facilities as schools and shops. Antonia and Thomas had joined a small class of children in the house of a fellow Christ Church don, Alec Carr-Saunders. He and his wife, Teresa, lived at Water Eaton Manor, an Elizabethan mansion a few miles north of Oxford. The house had considerably more rooms than occupants and the Carr-Saunders were therefore faced with the prospect of receiving evacuees. Rather than take in strangers, they offered a home to the Pakenham and to the Taylor households – Frank Taylor, another Christ Church don, was currently living at Cowley with his wife and two sons. The proposal was, therefore, that the Water Eaton household expand to include three young Pakenhams, two Taylor children and Edmund, Flora and Nicholas Carr-Saunders, and their respective nannies. Elizabeth found this a tempting offer: not only would it solve the problem of driving the children out to Water Eaton for their lessons each day, but it would also provide companionship and support for her while Frank was away.

They decided to accept the Carr-Saunders' hospitality. The contents of Singletree, including china, bed linen and kitchen equipment, was turned over to the Oxford city council, who took up the tenancy on the house and used it for evacuees. During the early part of the war Singletree was occupied by a group of blind Jews who had been evacuated from the East End of London. The new tenants had difficulty in their strange new surroundings and all the china was smashed in their heroic attempts to wash up in an unfamiliar sink.

Before moving into Water Eaton Elizabeth decided on a holiday for all the family at Bernhurst, where Frank would join her and the children. She found him exhausted by the rigours of camp life. Frank's normal facility for sleep had deserted him in the presence of eleven other men under canvas. Bernhurst gave them all a brief and badly needed respite, but Frank had to return to barracks near Banbury in mid-August, while Elizabeth, Jean, Antonia, Thomas and Paddy set off for their new home in Water Eaton. With the declaration of war Frank was persuaded that he could offer better service as an officer in the Oxford and Buckinghamshire Light Infantry – a change that did little to raise his morale, although the responsibility for teaching French to the troops provided some solace.

Sitting alone in the great hall of the old house, Elizabeth heard her cousin, Neville Chamberlain, announce that the country was at war – a war, he said, that might continue for three years. The pronouncement induced '. . . a rare sensation of total discouragement and depression' (*The Pebbled Shore*, p.

192). Had she known the step that Frank was now contemplating her gloom would have deepened. He had long been considering the possibility of joining the Roman Catholic Church, and the outbreak of war precipitated a decision.

Everything that Frank has undertaken, from joining the Labour Party to supporting prisoners and campaigning against pornography, has been at the prompting of conscience. As an undergraduate he had known Martin D'Arcy, the eminent Jesuit and Master of Campion Hall, the Jesuit house of studies in Oxford. In 1931 D'Arcy published *The Nature of Belief,* which made a considerable appeal to Frank. Campion Hall in Brewer Street, a couple of minutes from Christ Church, became a frequent haunt of his; here he had long discussions with Father D'Arcy, under whose direction he began to read theology and to attend Sunday mass at the Franciscan church in the Iffley Road, making no attempt to hide his activities from Elizabeth. For at least a year before taking the final step he had been held back by a lack of absolute conviction. The essential leap of faith finally seems to have been precipitated by the outbreak of war.

When it became known that the battalion was to be sent abroad, Frank received a pressing letter from Evelyn Waugh, urging him to come to a decision. 'Discussion can become a pure luxury,' Evelyn concluded. 'This is no time for a soldier to delay' (from Frank Longford's *Born to Believe,* p. 116). Thus prompted he sought formal instruction in the Roman Catholic faith from the Franciscans in Iffley Road, Martin D'Arcy himself being in the States. In January 1940 he learnt that the regiment was about to be sent to the Isle of Wight, which was generally believed to be a staging-post for France. This was considered a good enough reason for him to be received into the Roman Catholic Church without further delay. He spent a night in the Franciscan community and on the following morning attended mass and received communion before setting off for Water Eaton to break the news.

Elizabeth was shocked and deeply distressed both by Frank's conversion and still more by the secrecy surrounding it.[5] She believed at this stage that interfering priests would come between herself and Frank, that their children would be disadvantaged by anti-Catholic prejudice and that Frank's career would be similarly damaged. Worst of all, he would be sucked into an alien community from which she would be excluded.

Frank knew Elizabeth better than to argue; and at least she had not threatened to take the children and walk out on him. Elizabeth admits that to an extent her deep hurt and anger were stoked by the determination to live up to the reaction expected by Frank and her family. She was, however, able to convince herself that Frank had chosen the best way of breaking the news. 'I began to realize that even the secrecy of his final step had been the lesser of two evils for both of us. If he had warned me beforehand I should have felt bound to use every weapon in my armoury to dissuade him, and might have worked myself up into saying things that I did not really mean' (*The Pebbled Shore*, p. 197). Frank returned to his regiment, where his conversion did little to help him cope with army life. For Elizabeth the demands of 'community living' in Water Eaton under wartime conditions left little time for brooding.

6

Problems of War

Petrol rationing imposed considerable restraints on the Carr-Saunders, Pakenham and Taylor household. During term-time the governess and two additional children had to be brought out from Oxford and driven home each evening. There was not even a shop within walking distance, let alone a village. Before the outbreak of war Teresa Carr-Saunders had been experimenting with farming. In 1939 she stepped up her efforts to make the manor self-sufficient. She had a variety of livestock including ponies, pigs, donkeys, cattle and chickens, all of which tended to escape into the garden or even the house. Recapture, especially after dark and during the black-out, was far from easy. John Taylor, eight years old at the time, vividly recalls[1] Teresa Carr-Saunders' efforts to shoo out a row of chickens that had perched along the back of a silk damask sofa in the Elizabethan hall they used as the drawing room. She eventually dislodged the birds, but the furnishings were stained with droppings and ornaments had been smashed.

Even more disastrous was the fate of a hundred day-old chicks. Having to go out for the day, Teresa left careful instructions that the water container must not be put inside the birds' pen – if they needed to drink they could reach the container through the wire mesh. The children, convinced that the little creatures were unable to satisfy their thirst, brought the water container into the chickens' pen, with the result that all but a handful were drowned.

Water Eaton offered boundless enchantment for the children: the house was even supposed to have its own ghost – an officer who, according to legend, had shot himself in the attic during the First World War. A khaki-clad figure was seen by one of the nannies who assumed (wrongly) that Frank Pakenham had come home on unexpected leave. In the garden was an ancient private chapel and several outbuildings, while beyond the wall a water meadow led down to the river Cherwell. In the spring of 1940, inspired by their romantic surroundings, Antonia Pakenham and John Taylor, aged seven and eight, set out to elope by water, but the river was high with spring rains, their punt hit a bridge and the 'happy couple' were forced to abandon ship.

Elizabeth was still able to drive to Birmingham regularly to visit her King's Norton constituency. The journey had become increasingly hazardous, as car headlights had to be dimmed and the roads were blacked out. At home her major contribution to the household lay in teaching Latin and English to the ten children (two came by day to join the eight living at the manor) in one of the outbuildings, which had been converted for use as a classroom. Her lessons were sufficiently entertaining to be remembered half a century later. Making use of the textbook *Latin With Laughter* (by Sidney Frankenburg, published by Heinemann in 1931), she introduced relay races in which 'passing' the correct word took the place of passing the baton. Like her mother, she had read to the children from the earliest age, beginning with the Beatrix Potter books and graduating to *The Story of Rome* (by Norwood Young, published by Dent, 1926), which Antonia and Thomas listened to when they were six and five. J. R. R. Tolkien's *The Hobbit* (published by George Allen & Unwin in 1937), which she now read to the Water Eaton children, proved so popular that it dominated their games (*The Pebbled Shore*, p. 193). Dividing into teams, the 'baddies' were Gollums, named after Tolkien's monster, and the 'goodies' were the heroic Bellums, which they took from their knowledge of Latin.

In December 1941 conscription was extended to women between the ages of twenty and thirty, who could choose between the auxiliary services or 'war work' in factories or on the land. Meanwhile Teresa Carr-Saunders still had domestic help. But Regina, one of her two Polish maids, became depressed and ran away – possibly because the increased work in the enlarged household, coupled with the fall of Poland, had pushed her beyond endurance. She was eventually found by the police on Didcot station wearing Elizabeth's camel-hair coat, which the police allowed her to keep, because Elizabeth, despite the difficulty of replacing the coat in wartime, refused to press charges.

Although the war had seriously disrupted Elizabeth's life, she was coping; Frank, on the other hand, was finding the army so stressful that he became physically ill. Within a week of arriving in the Isle of Wight he had succumbed to such a severe attack of gastric 'flu that he was sent to the Manchester Street nursing home in London, where Elizabeth and many friends managed to visit. Although he made what appeared to be a rapid recovery and was able to return to his regiment, he fell ill again within weeks and was back in the nursing home by the end of March 1940. It had become obvious, not least to the army, that mental strain was exacerbating if not actually causing Frank's physical problems and that he was undergoing a complete mental breakdown. He spent several weeks in the nursing home until by May he was well enough to join Elizabeth at Bernhurst, where she was taking a break with the children. There he was informed by the adjutant that there would be no difficulty about his going before a medical board, which would in all likelihood lead to a discharge, as proved to be the case. Frank reluctantly returned to civilian life, joining his family at Water Eaton. In May 1940 the voluntary Home Guard, originally called the Local Defence Volunteer Reserve Force, was formed in response to the German blitzkrieg on the Low Countries and France and the consequent threat of German invasion. Men between the ages of seventeen and sixty-five who had been excused military service could enrol. Within twenty-four hours a quarter of a million had enrolled; by the end of June the figure had risen to one and a half million. Joining the Home Guard provided Frank with the opportunity to play some active part in the war effort and brought him some comfort for what he has always seen as his failure in the army.

For many it has become virtually impossible to dissociate the Home Guard from the British TV comedy *Dad's Army*. In Frank's case, the element of farce is inescapable, for he became a victim of incompetence confounded. Not only was he shot in the foot by one of his own company, but the doctor who dressed the wound stitched a piece of sock into it, bringing the hapless Frank close to losing his foot.

The invasion scare that followed the fall of France in 1940 led to severe restriction of movement in areas around the south coast. Bernhurst, thirteen miles from Hastings, lay in one of the villages that had been declared a Restricted Zone, and was therefore closed to all but permanent residents. As the house was no longer accessible, the Pakenhams turned Bernhurst over to the government; a siren was mounted on its roof and Nissen huts were dotted around the garden. The house was used at first as a debriefing centre for captured enemy airmen and later as a base for the Canadian army, who rigged up pipes to provide themselves with showers and established a laundry in the basement. Mrs Pope ('Popey'), who had been Great-Aunt Caroline Pakenham's housekeeper and had stayed on at Bernhurst, now joined Elizabeth in Oxford, where she was house-hunting once again.

Water Eaton had become too isolated for the family. Thomas and Antonia had outgrown the skills of a governess and now

needed to go to school. In addition, the long bicycle ride from
Water Eaton to the Home Guard headquarters in Oxford was
becoming too taxing for Frank. Furthermore, Elizabeth was
expecting her fourth child in a few months. A house was
urgently needed. Elizabeth discovered 8 Chadlington Road,
which was next door to the Dragon preparatory school and
was in many ways ideal, despite the fact that north Oxford was
a Conservative heartland. By coincidence Elizabeth had lodged
at number 10, the house next door, during her final term at
Oxford; here Frank had dreamt that he would find her and he
had done so. Elizabeth and Popey moved into 8 Chadlington
Road on 9th July, to prepare for the rest of the family and for
the new baby who, according to Dr Helena Wright's theory,
should be a girl. Judith was born on Thomas's seventh birthday,
14th August 1940, having given the family just enough time to
settle into their new home.

Judith's birth coincided with the beginning of the Battle of
Britain and although Oxford escaped regular raids there were
a number of scares. On one occasion Elizabeth and Popey went
to the local shops, leaving eight-year-old Antonia in charge of
Thomas, Paddy and baby Judith. They had not been gone long
when the sirens sounded. Rushing back, Elizabeth found
Antonia sitting calmly in the cellar with Thomas and Paddy
beside her and the new baby on her lap. As the bombardment
became more intense, German bombers passed overhead, en
route for the Midlands. Hearing the ominous throb of their
engines Elizabeth decided that Judith should sleep on the
ground floor, and that because of the night feeds, she and Frank
must move down also. Jean and the rest of the children would
continue to sleep upstairs. The dining room, which Frank had
been using as a study, was turned into their bedroom and the
revolving hatch connecting the room to the kitchen provided
an ideal place of safety for Judith's carrycot. As she rearranged
the rooms Elizabeth created what she called her 'chamber of
horrors', a bookshelf standing in the darkest hall corner, to the

bottom of which she banished Frank's loathsome Catholic books. Not long afterwards, Elizabeth was in the garden with the four children when a blazing plane crashed on to a neighbouring cottage, wiping out the family who lived there. Elizabeth saw the plane descending and barely had time to run with the children to the house before the deafening impact.

By 1941 food rationing was becoming severe and, in an attempt to reduce arguments, Elizabeth decreed that the three older children should have their individual butter dishes, labelled with their names. Certain foods such as biscuits and dried or tinned food, if they could be found, were from 1941 subject to a 'points' system, allowing for an element of personal choice. Although the London blitz was raging, Antonia, aged nine, was travelling each week to a Harley Street consultant for back treatment. On her return journey she was commissioned to do the 'points' shopping at Selfridges, since the London shops were generally better provisioned. Elizabeth relied increasingly on her eldest child, especially after the departure of Jean, who joined the Women's Royal Naval Reserve in July 1941, having been with the Pakenhams for five years.

Shortly after the move to Chadlington Road, Antonia started at the Dragon School (which was almost next door), where she was to be followed by Thomas, Paddy and Judith. 'She-Dragons' were outnumbered ten to one by the boys, and were expected to undertake the same classes and sports, while parents were urged to take a keen interest in all school activities: Elizabeth needed little encouragement.

By 1942 Paddy, aged five, was showing signs of being particularly gifted in classics. Elizabeth began to teach him Latin and gave him an English translation of *The Odyssey* when he was six; two years later she began to teach him Greek. It may have been Paddy's intelligence that led to boredom, which in turn accounted for his destructiveness – a trait that maddened Elizabeth. One day she caught Paddy stripping the flowers from her lavender bushes. He managed to break her fountain pen – an essential tool and irreplaceable in wartime – and later he took a hammer to one of the pilasters on the verandah. Perhaps there were times when he was as much sinned against as sinning: Paddy has never forgotten his mother dragging him off the playground to finish his breakfast at the very moment he had succeeded in getting a rare turn with a cricket bat.

Elizabeth was known to be a strict mother holding to specific rules: no bullying, no skipping homework, no fetching food from the larder between meals, no leaving the table until everyone had finished and no reading in bed. In theory she abhorred smacking or hitting a child, but with the three older ones practice could be less perfect than precept. Sometimes she asked Frank to administer punishment, but he felt that it was inhuman for a man weighing eleven and a half stone to hit a child weighing five and a half (*The Pebbled Shore*, p. 210) and delivered no more than token chastisement. Paddy maintains that his father's half-hearted blows were something of a joke in comparison with those of his mother.

In the 1950s, when Elizabeth began to write articles for the *Daily Express* on the rearing of children, she firmly repudiated any form of corporal punishment, and she has now come to believe that her younger children, who she very rarely smacked, were less violent than the others. As they grew older the children were punished for misdemeanours by being asked to read a book or learn poetry by heart; they also had to recite verses from the Bible on a Sunday before being given their pocket money. As well as reading aloud to her children Elizabeth made some attempt to supervise their own reading and to guide their choice of wireless programmes: this was quite simple when the only wireless was in the drawing room. Books were harder to monitor and Elizabeth had mixed feelings about censorship. She cared deeply about her children's reading, while adhering to the principle of their right to freedom of choice. Thus Antonia got away with reading 'penny dreadfuls' borrowed from Popey's grown-up daughter, Alice, who had borrowed them from the public library.

At the end of the 1950s, when Elizabeth's youngest daughter, Catherine, was a young teenager, *Lolita*, by Vladimir Nabokov, was published. The book, which tells of a middle-aged professor's infatuation for a young girl, was lauded by some as great art and condemned by others as pornographic. A copy was given to Elizabeth and, while she would not have dreamt of putting it into Catherine's hands, she could not bring herself to ban the book. Compromising, she wrapped *Lolita* in a plain cover and put it at the bottom of an out-of-the-way shelf. Here Catherine found it and, as she confessed to her mother in later years, started to read it, but was too bored to proceed further than the opening chapters.

The difficulties of running a house and controlling the children were complicated by the daily problem of making the rations go round. Air-raids continued, especially in London where throughout 1941 Frank was working with William Beveridge on the social report that was to come out at the end of the year.[2] (The first Beveridge report, 'Social Insurance and Allied Services', was published in 1942, and the second, 'Full Employment in a Free Society', in 1944.) He wrote daily letters to Elizabeth, who was startled by the suggestion of the possibility of a move to Ireland. Edward had offered Pakenham to Frank provided he paid for the furniture. Elizabeth shared Frank's devotion to Ireland, but could not imagine how his career or her own could be continued if they were living there. Nevertheless, knowing what it would mean to Frank to live at Pakenham, she decided that she would not oppose the change, but in the event Edward withdrew his offer.

Although Frank returned to Oxford for weekends, the brief days together were not always without friction. Antonia remembers a row about the repainting of the house. As they were always short of money, Elizabeth was unenthusiastic about repainting; Frank was not only in favour but wanted the house painted blue, a colour Elizabeth dislikes on political grounds: she was sufficiently provoked to throw a book at his head.

Moreover, Elizabeth was again in trouble with the Labour Party. When the coalition government had been formed under Winston Churchill in 1940, a political truce had been agreed between the major parties, who were expected to abandon their differences and use their combined energy to win the war. On the death or resignation of a member, the replacement would be from the same party, in order to maintain the agreed balance. The Conservative MP for the King's Norton division of Birmingham, Ronald Cartland, was killed on active service in 1940. Before there could be a by-election, the King's Norton divisional Labour Party issued a manifesto criticising the policy of the Conservatives. Because they had not put forward their own candidate, Elizabeth, they maintained that their manifesto had not broken the truce. The National Executive of the Labour Party, however, insisted that truce meant the cessation of all political controversy for the duration of the war. Therefore King's Norton had broken the truce both in spirit and in action; they had also deliberately failed to consult either their Birmingham colleagues or the National Executive before issuing the manifesto. Elizabeth, with the full backing of King's Norton, insisted that the exact requirements of the truce were far from clear and that in any event Labour principles and policies must be publicised in order to prepare for post-war social reform.

In hindsight, a minor issue may appear to have been blown out of proportion, but at the time issues of consultation, loyalty and the autonomy of local parties were hotly debated. The National Executive demanded an apology from King's Norton and a promise of strict future adherence to the truce. King's Norton refused and was therefore suspended from affiliation to the party. In the Labour archives in Manchester is a copy of a long letter from Elizabeth to the National Executive, setting out the King's Norton case. She concludes by asking for clarification of her position as a member of the Oxford City Labour

Party and that of the Fabian Society.[3] After much argument and indignation, the suspension of King's Norton was withdrawn and the matter dropped.

As her letter indicates, Elizabeth was consistently active in local Labour Party affairs; Chadlington Road, like Singletree, became a venue for local meetings, held, whenever possible, in the garden. The children played while the women held their discussions, sitting in a circle making baby shoes, patchwork quilts, dolls' clothes and anything else that would sell at the annual bazaar. Despite her political activities, Elizabeth was in many ways a conventional mother; she spent a great deal of time with her children, teaching them, taking them for walks around the park with her great friend, Bice Fawcett, and organising summer holidays.

As Bernhurst was in a restricted zone, she frequently took the children to her parents' house in Crockham Hill, Kent, Larksfield (to which they had moved in 1930 when their lease expired on Lynchfield) or to Frank's sister, Pansy Lamb, and her family at Coombe Bissett in Wiltshire. There Elizabeth was known as Aunt Beezibum, an early attempt at 'Elizabeth', a name she readily adopted and used as a signature on post cards to her nieces. Much of the south coast being designated a restricted zone, the possibilities for seaside holidays were greatly reduced during the war. Elizabeth, with her love of sea and sand, managed a holiday for the family in Cornwall at Porthscatho in the summer of 1941, and in 1942 she took them to a hotel in St Just.

Frank's work on the Beveridge report – where he was responsible for publicity – was highly successful and Elizabeth's spat with the Labour Party NEC, while doing no serious damage, had advanced her standing with the radicals in the party. Antonia and Thomas were doing well at the Dragon, where Paddy would soon join them. When Judith was a year old Elizabeth began to experience 'a baby itch again' (*The Pebbled Shore*, p. 210). In an interview with the *Daily Express* in 1990 she recalled that 'every time the baby became a toddler I wanted to have another one'.

Although she was now happily expecting her fifth child, 1941 was a year of deep sadness caused by the death of Elizabeth's brother, Roger. Shortly before the war Roger had been found to be suffering from a brain tumour. His death at the age of thirty was a severe blow to Elizabeth, her parents and the whole family. Visiting him in hospital for the last time, she realised that she was no longer as close to Roger as she had been when they had been children. Reflecting upon this subsequently, she became painfully aware of the superficiality of her final conversation with him. 'We talked of this and that, of his future, all optimistically, nothing truthfully' (*The Pebbled Shore*, p. 222). Elizabeth was unable to escape the uncomfortable truth that she herself lacked the inner certainty that could have comforted her dying brother.

Frank had now been a Catholic for the best part of two years and many of his friends were surprised, not to say critical, that he had 'failed' to convert Elizabeth. Frank, however, understood her better than anyone else and knew that if Elizabeth was ever to become a Catholic it would have to be on the basis of intellectual conviction and faith, rather than because of her undoubted devotion to himself. He was also aware that any attempt to influence her might well strengthen her opposition. Religion was not discussed at home although Elizabeth had begun to take Antonia and Thomas to church. She hated the moment when, having all set out together, they had to part: Frank going on to mass at St Aloysius while she took the children to St Paul's, the High Anglican church in Walton Street.

In December 1941, to demonstrate her pride in Frank's part in the Beveridge report, Elizabeth accompanied him to mass at St Aloysius. This was the first mass that she had ever attended but, as the priest devoted the whole of his sermon to a tirade against Beveridge and all that the report stood for, it might well have been the last. The priest's attitude to social reform confirmed her belief that the Catholic Church had no social conscience and always supported dictators against the people, as proved by its role in the Spanish Civil War. Her prejudice was deep-seated: in addition to the anti-Catholic books of her upbringing, she had a clear memory of her reaction to her father's explanation of the Anglo-Catholic doctrine of transubstantiation. In her teens she had not been able to understand how adults could be so superstitious as to believe that after the priest had spoken the words of consecration, bread and wine 'became' the body and blood of Christ.

Years later one of her friends told Elizabeth that she felt an out-and-out hypocrite because she prayed to God only when she was desperate. Elizabeth replied, 'That's what God's for' (Elizabeth's diary). She knew what she was talking about. When Frank was in London during the worst of the blitz, she tried for the first time in twenty years to pray for him (recalled in Frank Longford's *Born to Believe*, p. 120). Shaken by Roger's death, she was finding her agnostic position increasingly untenable; even the verses that she had composed and sent to her mother in memory of Roger ended with the line, 'The end is not yet', evincing, perhaps, a wistful longing for belief in a life after death.

Elizabeth's faltering progress towards Christian belief seems to have followed what she conceived to be the children's religious needs rather than any urging by Frank. Unlike Elizabeth and her brothers and sister, Antonia, Thomas and Paddy were all baptised. As Judith was the first of the children to be born after Frank's conversion, Elizabeth had even considered allowing her to be baptised into the Roman Catholic Church, but decided against it. Six of the eight children were therefore baptised into the Church of England. At this time Elizabeth described herself as an 'indifferentist', a word she coined to describe her total lack of interest in faith or belief. Thus, for her, baptism was a social rather than a religious event and while she could not bring herself to teach the children about Jesus, she was happy for their nanny, Jean, to do so. She might not have faith herself, but she did not want her children deprived of the opportunity of receiving it.

Antonia and Thomas, aged nine and eight, were ready for confirmation in the Church of England. On the advice of Muriel Williams, a Dragon mother and wife of the Dean of Christ Church, Elizabeth sent them to be prepared for confirmation by Father Favell, the Anglo-Catholic rector of St Paul's. There candles, bells and incense were a part of normal worship, as was the reservation of the blessed sacrament. 'To me High Church piety had become more attractive than Low Church simplicity,' commented Elizabeth on her volte-face from her Unitarian upbringing (*The Pebbled Shore*, p. 221). In hindsight the change seems to have been foreshadowed by her reaction to the Thanksgiving service at the Austin Friars church in the City of London at the end of the First World War, a service that had moved her deeply.

On 11th May 1942 Rachel, third daughter and fifth child, was born in Chadlington Road. She, too, travelled in the back of the car to the constituency in Birmingham, where eyebrows were raised by some Labour Party members scandalised at the growing number of Pakenham children. Those who were more kindly disposed thought that as Elizabeth already had two boys and two girls, Rachel must have been a mistake. 'If you don't make mistakes, you don't make anything' was a popular Labour maxim, so no comment was officially made, but when Elizabeth became pregnant again within a year of Rachel's birth, a delicate mission fell upon Harold Nash. He had to warn her that some supporters were insisting that Elizabeth must guarantee that there would be no more children. Without that guarantee they would withdraw support on the grounds that such a large family would prevent her from fulfilling the demands made on a Member of Parliament.

Elizabeth was furious: no one was going to dictate how many children she should have. The baby Elizabeth was now carrying was very much wanted. She planned to have a boy and had followed Dr Helena Wright's advice. Moreover, she had taken on a mother's help, Liz Butler, a young married woman with a six-month-old baby of her own, in order to ensure the necessary domestic help.

Harold Nash did not share Elizabeth's confidence in her ability to manage both her constituency and her growing family. In October 1943, a month before the baby was due, the Executive Committee was to meet to discuss Elizabeth's position. If she was to remain prospective Labour candidate for King's Norton she would have to address the concerns of party members. To persuade her to do this Harold Nash came to Oxford in August, with three senior Committee members to work out a strategy for the critical meeting. Although Elizabeth was prepared to be conciliatory she was not going to promise that this would be her last child. At the meeting, Elizabeth, eight months pregnant, literally carried all before her in a rousing speech, to which the committee responded with a vote of confidence endorsing her as their prospective candidate.

Michael was born on 3rd November 1943. This was the only birth from which Frank was absent: he was in the north of England with Beveridge, now pursuing a new inquiry into full employment. Shortly after Frank's return, the author and scientist Solly Zuckerman came to see him at Chadlington Road. A distracted Frank, surrounded by a tribe of small children, opened the door to him. 'Come in, come in, or they'll all fall out,' he implored.

Christmas 1943 was not a success. Elizabeth was worn out. Since the birth of Judith in 1940 she had been constantly either pregnant or nursing a baby; on top of the exhaustion she was suffering from migraine, piles, sinusitis and depression. Having successfully made her stand to the King's Norton Labour Executive, she now began to find the idea of resignation increasingly attractive, and was drawing closer to a decision that would put an end to her political career.

When the Executive Committee met again on 9th January

1944, the members were surprised and indignant to find themselves faced with her change of heart. Elizabeth had decided to resign and had written to tell them so. This was a volte-face, ironically set in motion by the Committee's raising the whole question in the first place. The decision was precipitated by her own health, but additionally the late-night drives between Birmingham and Oxford were dangerous in the blackout and becoming increasingly burdensome. On one occasion, with Rachel in the back of the unheated car and the windscreen opaque with frost, Elizabeth had had to drive with the window open. Neither she nor Rachel came to any harm during that long, intensely cold journey, but it seemed increasingly irresponsible to expose another tiny baby to such risks.

Elizabeth was also concerned about Frank. Convinced as she was that King's Norton would be won by Labour, there was no such certainty about Oxford City. The industrial and solidly Labour areas of Cowley and Headington, to which he should have been able to look for support, were in the neighbouring Tory rural constituency of South Oxfordshire. The boundaries were due to be altered, but such a change was unlikely in time of war. Had she not resigned it was more than possible that after the next general election Elizabeth would have won King's Norton, while Frank lost Oxford City. '... I would be sent up to Westminster with a mandate to set the Thames on fire, while Frank stayed behind to keep the home fires burning ...' (*The Pebbled Shore*, p. 218).

Exhaustion, war-weariness and depression had also contributed to a rare loss of nerve. Elizabeth had begun to wonder whether she could really do justice to her six young children and to thousands of constituents. She had always maintained that it was possible for a woman to run her family and her career, but in her own case husband and children had to come first. Resignation therefore seemed inevitable. The step had to be taken at once in order to give the Executive

Committee time to select another candidate. She put her case,
faced the committee with a dignified farewell speech in which
she begged them to believe that her six years as their candidate
had not been wasted for the Labour Party in King's Norton,
and resigned.

7

Changing Directions

After six years of constant, exhilarating work at King's Norton, lack of activity outside the home cast a pall over the beginning of 1944, a difficult year that was to be plagued by illness. Seven-year-old Paddy was the first to succumb. In the spring he had developed earache, which he bore so stoically that, until his temperature soared, Elizabeth did not realise that he was seriously ill. Paddy had an infected mastoid requiring immediate surgery; he was on the danger list for several anxious days. Penicillin, discovered in 1928, was in 1944 in sufficient supply only for treatment of service personnel; it was not in general use until 1959/60.

The long-awaited invasion of France on 6th June brought hope that the end of the war might be finally in sight and this did much to lift the general gloom in Chadlington Road. In July Elizabeth had a stiff shoulder and arranged for a massage. The masseuse was exceedingly vigorous and shortly after Elizabeth returned home she began to haemorrhage. The doctor who attended her told her that she had miscarried twins. Elizabeth was both saddened and indignant; she was still nursing eight-month-old Michael and was not aware that she was pregnant again. In August she had hardly recovered when Frank went down in his usual dramatic style with an attack of lumbago. He had tried to get out of the train only to double up with pain and fall out on to the platform. Mindful of his mother's arthritis, Elizabeth was always alarmed when Frank succumbed to any form of rheumatism, but he recovered.

Family trials turned Elizabeth's mind to spiritual matters. She recalled the experience of reading the four gospels straight through for the first time in 1941 as a result of the death of her brother, Roger. As a child she had never questioned her mother's interpretation of Jesus as a good man, specially called, but not God incarnate, not the second person of the Blessed Trinity. As a young adult she had discarded even this minimal belief without further thought. Nearly twenty years on, she now found herself studying the gospels more seriously as her personal faith gradually evolved. St John's gospel led her to a belief in Jesus as God. The 'meek and mild' Jesus of her childhood – a Jesus who seemed to lack all relevance to the unemployed or exploited – gave way to the perception of an indignant Jesus, who thirsted for justice and caused mayhem by driving out the temple money-lenders and overturning their tables. This was a Jesus whom Elizabeth would have expected to find alongside the comrades on their hunger marches.

Once her intellectual curiosity had been aroused, Elizabeth attempted to satisfy it by turning to Frank's theological books, those 'loathsome' volumes previously cast into her 'chamber of horrors'. *True Humanism* by Jacques Maritain (first published in 1936 and in English in 1938) made a significant impression.[1] According to Maritain humanism was a system of belief that centred itself on God, not, as she had previously believed, one that made human beings the ultimate measure. This book drove a coach and four through the preconceptions on which Elizabeth had previously based her objections to the Catholic faith. 'It was through Maritain that my worst demon was exorcised: dislike of the Catholic Church for its part in the Spanish Civil War' (*The Pebbled Shore*, p. 223). Her growing faith is reflected in the letter written to her mother in August 1943 to comfort her on what should have been Roger's thirty-second birthday: '. . . Now I firmly believe in immortality, even some kind of personal reunion, though I suppose with our finite minds we can never quite conceive how it can be. But the great thing is – that it will be.'

In addition to her study of the gospels, and prompted by anxiety either for Frank or for the children, Elizabeth had on occasion attempted to pray. Frank had no inhibitions and would often drop to his knees at home or in his office, but Elizabeth found prayer both difficult and a very private activity; for some time she would not pray in front of Frank. The dangers of the blitz and Paddy's illness had driven her to persist, although she began by seeking the privacy of the Anglo-Catholic St Paul's, where Antonia and Thomas were being prepared for confirmation by the Rector, Father Favell.

Striding through the streets to his church in his long black cassock, the tall, handsome Father Favell was an impressive sight. In July 1944 Antonia and Thomas were confirmed by Dr Kirk, the Bishop of Oxford, and a few weeks later Father Favell began to instruct Elizabeth whom he baptised on 1st December. Frank was delighted and even managed to be present when she made her first communion on the following day, although he had had to secure special permission to attend this Anglican act of worship (since, until the mid-1960s, Catholics were not permitted to attend services of other denominations). Some three weeks later Elizabeth attended midnight mass at St Paul's and found the service deeply moving.

After Frank had been received into the Catholic Church in 1940, religion had become one of the few topics never mentioned, but once Elizabeth embarked on her study, there were constant and lively religious discussions. Elizabeth had, however, made up her mind that she would never follow Frank into the Roman Catholic Church during her father's lifetime; she was resigned, therefore, to continued disagreement in some areas of their lives.

This decision was based on an 'unusually critical letter from my usually gentle mother' written in 1940 (*The Pebbled Shore,*

p. 235) in which Mrs Harman demonstrated all the prejudice that until then Elizabeth had shared. Her mother had written of the danger that interfering priests would pose to Elizabeth's marriage and of the disadvantage that Roman Catholicism would inflict on the children's careers and prospects. Elizabeth assumed that the letter expressed her father's views as much as those of her mother. Years later, after the death of her mother in 1960, Elizabeth reread her parents' love letters. She realised for the first time how much it had cost her father to give up his belief in the divinity of Jesus, the sacrifice demanded by her Unitarian mother; and she began to wonder whether she had been mistaken about her father's reaction to her conversion. Her own beliefs had by then brought a measure of peace and strength and she regretted that her brief stay in the Anglican Church had prevented her from exploring issues of faith with her father. Perhaps he might have been able to talk to her mother in a way she could not. She felt guilty because she believed that she had failed to give spiritual support either to her mother or to her brother Roger.

But the spring of 1945 was no time for private regrets, for war in Europe was drawing to a close. The Russian advance on Berlin was heralding certain victory; this would be followed by the end of the political truce in Britain and a general election in which the parties were free to campaign once more for their own candidates. War with Germany ended on 8th May, Parliament was dissolved on 15th June and a general election was called for 5th July 1945. Although not herself a candidate, Elizabeth was fully occupied in supporting Frank in the Oxford City constituency, where he was at a disadvantage. As Elizabeth had feared, the constituency boundaries had not yet been redrawn and he was denied the support of the numerous Labour voters from the working-class districts of Cowley and Headington.

Elizabeth has described the 1945 election as 'the second most significant election of the century... [which] became an avalanche of victories for Labour' (*The Pebbled Shore*, p. 226; she rated the Liberal landslide of 1906 first, and the Conservative victory of 1979 third in importance). This was a triumph from which Frank and Elizabeth were excluded. In Oxford City Frank was opposed by their old friend Quintin Hogg, standing as a Conservative, and by the Liberal Antony Norman, who was actively supported by William Beveridge. In view of all Frank's work for Beveridge, Elizabeth saw this as something akin to betrayal. Quintin Hogg, as a friendly gesture, dropped in to Chadlington Road one afternoon before the campaign was under way. Antonia and Thomas were now both away at boarding-school, and when eight-year-old Paddy was asked to fetch the extra teacup he refused, in the belief that to succour 'the enemy' would compromise his loyalty to his father.

But neither Paddy's loyalty nor Elizabeth's pony-cart, filled with her children and covered with election posters, could save Frank. He was among the minority of defeated Labour candidates and it was particularly galling that the seat for which he had been originally adopted, Birmingham West, had succeeded in returning a Labour member. While the party under Clement Attlee was celebrating the first majority Labour government to take office, Elizabeth and Frank remained on the sidelines with no part to play beyond that of applauding the triumph of their friends. Hugh Gaitskell, Douglas Jay, Evan Durbin, Patrick Gordon Walker, Richard Crossman and Aidan Crawley were among those who had been returned to Westminster. At King's Norton, from which she had resigned, Raymond Blackburn, the Labour candidate, was returned with a majority of over 1200. No one doubted that Elizabeth's years of work in the constituency had played a considerable part in this satisfactory result.

Visits from friends helped to dispel Elizabeth and Frank's feelings of isolation. Evan Durbin had known and respected Frank since their Oxford undergraduate days. He was determined to get him into Parliament and as Parliamentary

Private Secretary to the newly appointed Chancellor of the Exchequer, Hugh Dalton, he had every hope of success. Dalton was visiting the Cotswolds shortly after the result of the election was announced. Durbin was able to arrange a meeting in Burford with the Pakenhams, as a result of which Arthur Greenwood, the Lord Privy Seal, invited Frank to become his personal assistant. Although this was a humbler position than Elizabeth might have wished for Frank, the appointment reopened the door to the possibility of political office.

Durbin, however, had more ambitious plans for Frank, whom he wanted to see in the Lords, supporting Attlee's policies of nationalisation and the implementation of the Beveridge report on social insurance. Frank's work for Beveridge, coupled with his brilliant first and his acclaimed book *Peace by Ordeal*, had won him general respect with the party. It was believed that he would be an asset in the Lords where Labour's position could hardly have been weaker. There were few Labour peers, and of these several were too frail and elderly to provide reliable support. Unquestionably Attlee would have to nominate several new peers; Durbin could think of several good reasons why Frank should be one of them. He was not only extremely able, but was likely to inherit a peerage. (Frank's brother, Edward, was still childless at the age of forty-three.) Durbin's only doubt was whether Frank would accept such elevation.

Frank and Elizabeth wrestled with this possibility while walking round and round the cricket pitches of the Dragon School. Elizabeth was not attracted to the idea. Unlike Frank, she had not been brought up in a milieu in which membership of the Upper House was commonplace. Not only did the ultra-nonconformist Unitarians have a strong bias against the Establishment but Elizabeth had advocated abolition of the House of Lords in 1935 when she fought the Cheltenham seat for Labour. She was also concerned about the practical implications. She questioned whether, by becoming a peer, Frank would not be throwing away his chance of the highest positions in the state. As a peer he would never be Prime Minister, Foreign Secretary or Chancellor of the Exchequer. 'Lady Pakenham' would be a strange title for an abolitionist, but she gave little thought to her own position; all her concern was focused on Frank and his future.

Although he was aware of Elizabeth's position, Evan Durbin argued strongly in favour of Frank's acceptance: as a Roman Catholic was he not already barred from the premiership, even if he managed to get into the House of Commons at the next general election? Furthermore, it would probably be only a matter of time before Frank succeeded Edward Longford, who was not robust, and became a member of the House of Lords. (The Longford earldom was an Irish creation and therefore carried no seat in Westminster after the 1801 Act of Union, but the United Kingdom Barony of Silchester, an additional Pakenham peerage, which Frank would inherit on the death of Edward, entitled him to a seat in the Upper House.) This argument carried little weight for Elizabeth; of far greater importance was the fact that refusal of a peerage would leave Frank with no option but a return to academic life and exclusion from the 'real' world of politics. Unlike Elizabeth, Frank had no hesitation. If he accepted the proposed peerage there was the likelihood that he might become Leader of the House of Lords, with a seat in the Cabinet.[2]

For a brief interval politics were put aside for the celebrations of victory over Japan that brought the Second World War to an end on 15th August 1945. To Elizabeth's great joy her brother John returned almost at once from active service in Burma. John, at thirty-eight, was still a bachelor, and was impatient to marry and start a family. He appealed to Elizabeth to help him find a suitable wife. She responded by inviting him to the Victory Ball at the Oxford Town Hall to which she and Frank were taking a party of friends; David and Rachel Cecil had been invited and, for John, Anna Spicer, a radical young lawyer. The party was a great success and Elizabeth's reputation as a

Katherine Harman, 1905.

Nat Harman when he was a civilian
doctor in the Boer War, 1901.

Elizabeth (Betty) Harman,
aged 3, 1909.

Elizabeth, 1925.

Elizabeth Harman and Frank Pakenham are engaged, 1931.

Bride and groom, 3rd November 1931.

Elizabeth and Frank
on honeymoon in Ireland, 1931.

Elizabeth addressing a Labour Party
meeting at Banbury, 1935.

Kevin helping his mother, 1949.

On holiday at Bude, 1946. Left to right: Rachel, Judith, Elizabeth,
Michael, Antonia and Paddy.

At home in Hampstead, 1950. Left to right: Paddy, Thomas, Antonia, Catherine Rachel, Elizabeth, Kevin, Judith and Michael.

Frank and Elizabeth lunching at Bernhurst, 1951.

Catherine, aged 6, helping with the housework, 1952.

Four generations, 1957. Left to right: Antonia, Rebecca,
Katherine and Elizabeth.

Elizabeth at Larksfield,
her parents' home, 1955.

Judith's wedding, 1963. Left to right: Antonia,
Rachel, Elizabeth and Catherine.

Frank in Garter robes with Elizabeth, 1971.

Elizabeth on holiday in Corfu, 1979.

Elizabeth loves a party, 1980.

Frank and Elizabeth on their Golden Wedding, 1981.

Promoting *The Pebbled Shore*, 1986.

Four generations, 1987. Left to right: Flora Powell Jones,
Elizabeth holding Stella Powell Jones and Antonia.

Family group on Elizabeth's 90th birthday, 1996.
Left to right: Kate Pakenham, Chloe Billington, Alex Pakenham, Rose Billington
Elizabeth, Rachel, Clio Pakenham, Frank and Judith.

matchmaker was strengthened when Anna and John were married in the following spring.[3]

Frank decided, with Elizabeth's support, to accept the peerage. Thus on 16th October 1945, at the age of thirty-nine, he took his seat in the House of Lords as Baron Pakenham of Cowley. Elizabeth and Antonia were waiting in the chamber as, within minutes of his installation, Frank rose to answer questions on behalf of the government. With hindsight, Elizabeth would agree with the widely held view that Frank, as champion of the underdog and campaigner for unpopular causes, has exerted greater influence in the Upper Chamber than would have been possible in the House of Commons.

Frank became increasingly absorbed in the work of the Lords, and many friends were beginning their careers in the House of Commons, but Elizabeth was left behind in Oxford. She felt a sense of isolation and sadness for what might have been had she not abandoned her own political career. But she was now pregnant again, with her seventh child. Difficult as it had been to nurse her babies while travelling between Oxford and Birmingham, her situation at Westminster would have been worse. There were then only twenty-four women MPs, and even the acknowledgment of the need for a crèche lay many years in the future. It also so happened that her struggle to accept the loss of a political career was overshadowed by the deeper and more personal loss of her father.

On VE Day, just two months earlier, when Elizabeth was suffering from a severe attack of conjunctivitis, she had telephoned her father for professional advice. This was to be the last time that he could offer such help. At seventy-six he was worn out, having never fully recovered from a fall from a ladder during the previous year. He was taken to hospital for saline injections to restore his failing strength, but died later in the day. When Mrs Harman told her daughter of his misery at having to go to hospital, Elizabeth made up her mind that if she were ever responsible for the well-being of a dying person, she would do her utmost to ensure that that person could die at home. Grieving for her mother's loss, Elizabeth made Frank promise that he would outlive her.

Elizabeth was surprised by the depth of her own grief for her father. She had always been aware of the debt she owed him for many of her interests. Her ability to speak in public came largely from him, as did her artistic talents. A gifted ophthalmic surgeon, Nat Harman had been almost brutal in regard to the health of his own children. Strict, puritanical and parsimonious, he was casual to the point of neglect in his own dress. 'Who is that shabby old man?' enquired Nat's own brother-in-law at a family wedding.

In later age, however, Nat mellowed and, although he remained intolerant of noise, he could be endlessly patient with his grandchildren. He sent them miniature letters filled with news. These he folded into tiny matching envelopes made from scrap paper, on which he wrote and illustrated the address and a miniature stamp. At least one has survived, addressed to Paddy at Chadlington Road. A year or two before Nat's death, Frank had breakfasted with him in London and, struck by the change in him, wrote to Elizabeth (letter quoted in *The Pebbled Shore*, p. 235) telling her 'how popular a man he is likely to be when he is laying himself out to be pleasant. He was sweet about you.' As time wore on he became less tight-fisted, but he still had more to leave than any of the family expected. 'It was very nice. But why had he stinted us so obsessively in our childhood, when a somewhat gayer lifestyle would have been appreciated even more than his legacies could be now?' Elizabeth commented.

Grieving for her father, Elizabeth also experienced a sense of increased freedom in her search for meaningful religious belief, which, despite her recent baptism into the Church of England, was a continuing preoccupation. In September 1945, only two months after her father's death, she made her first visit to Blackfriars, the Dominican priory in Oxford. Gervase

Mathew, the priest to whom she was drawn, was the cousin of Robert Mathew, the eccentric student with whom she had shared lodgings in Grenoble, before she went up to Oxford.

The scholarly Gervase Mathew was in his own way hardly less eccentric than Robert; although a Roman Catholic priest, he was well known and loved among the High Anglicans of Oxford, including Father Favell who had so recently instructed Elizabeth. Father Gervase was a lecturer on Byzantine art, an expert on medieval English poetry and history with sufficient knowledge of ancient Greece to be invited to lecture on Hellenic cruises. He was also at home with the literary and religious world of C. S. Lewis, Charles Williams and J. R. R. Tolkien. Gervase Mathew was a Dominican whose political sympathies clearly lay to the left. This was a priest whose intellect, concerns and sympathies were akin to those of Elizabeth.

Thus while Frank was establishing himself at Westminster, Elizabeth was continuing her spiritual journey in Oxford. Systematic reading had already given her a sound grasp of Catholic doctrine. She was now ready to accept transubstantiation, a doctrine which in her youth she had regarded as mumbo-jumbo and the height of superstition. As a married woman, familiar with St John's 'You in me and I in you' (John 14:20), she found the concept more acceptable. She and Frank were indubitably one, while yet remaining essentially themselves. Furthermore, Gervase helped her to understand the mystery involved, as he explained that no chemical change took place in the elements of the bread and wine believed to be converted into the body and blood of Christ. The doctrine was not, for her, in conflict with rational belief.

Elizabeth was helped by Gervase Mathew's sensitive approach to the Church's position on the purpose of marriage and the condemnation of artificial birth control, which had created difficulties for so many. He admitted to her that his own parents' decision to sleep in separate rooms in order to avoid the conception of another child had damaged their relationship. Elizabeth, for her part, admitted the effectiveness of the 'safe period' method, which she had been practising for the last two years. In response to her problems with Black Popes⁴ and scandalous priests, Gervase used the analogy of pipes: whether a pipe be lead or gold, the purity of the water is not affected. He constantly emphasised the mystery of the Catholic faith, recalling the image of a firelit cave used by Plato in *The Republic*. Fire, burning with a flickering mysterious flame, casts light, which comes and goes, leaving obscure corners of the cave permanently in shadow.

Elizabeth had some difficulty with accepting Mary, the mother of Christ, a difficulty compounded by her old friend Anne Martelli, a 'cradle' Catholic, who told her to pray to Mary for special favours, explaining that it was 'easier and less presumptuous to approach Mary rather than going direct to the Almighty'. Elizabeth thought this sounded like 'going to the private secretary instead of the minister'. Conversely, the dogma of the bodily Assumption of Mary into heaven posed no problem; it seemed complimentary to women, redressing the tendency to feel shame or disgust for the flesh that had been a legacy of the third-century Manichaean heresy that everything sprang from two chief principles, light and darkness, or good and evil (*The Pebbled Shore*, pp. 237–9).

Elizabeth made her decision to become a Catholic early in 1946, a decision that was welcomed by many, but by none more than Frank. His solitary Sunday walk to St Aloysius, while Elizabeth and the children made their way to St Paul's in Walton Street, had played no small part in her decision. Frank undertook the uncomfortable task of explaining Elizabeth's change of heart to Dr Kirk, the Bishop of Oxford, who had so recently confirmed her in the Anglican Church. With no hint of reproach, Dr Kirk, demonstrating a truly advanced ecumenical spirit, wrote in a reassuring letter, 'I am certain that you are doing the only wise and right thing . . . Whilst a family that has no religion is the worst thing of all, a family of divided allegiances is in itself unnatural . . . So I rejoice that you are both to walk along the same path (with, I hope, the children too) even though it's not the same as mine.'

Dr Kirk's hope for the children was partially fulfilled on 7th April 1946 when Catherine Rose, Elizabeth's seventh child, was baptised by the Jesuit Fr William MacMullen, some weeks before Elizabeth's own reception. Among Catherine's sponsors were Peggy Attlee, Clement's niece, and Evelyn Waugh, who gave her a golden knife, fork and spoon.

Antonia, aged thirteen, and Thomas, aged twelve, were thought to be old enough to make up their own minds. 'Antonia is very devout and prays in a mumble of devotion with shut eyes,' Elizabeth had noted (in the baby record book) when the child was four. As soon as she knew of her mother's decision to become a Catholic, Antonia clamoured to change from the Godolphin School in Salisbury to St Mary's Convent, Ascot. Thomas, in hindsight at least, recalls the swift and seemingly frequent changes of religion with some cynicism. 'It was all very sudden. We moved very rapidly from nothing – high agnostic – to Anglicanism. Then we were told that we were no longer Anglo-Catholics, we were moving on again' (quoted in Peter Stanford's biography of Lord Longford).

In addition to Bishop Kirk's letter, Elizabeth also received a letter from Evelyn Waugh, which began, 'Please let me join the Saints and Angels in their chorus of welcome . . .'. The letter was all the more pleasing to Elizabeth for its marked contrast with the constant and not always friendly banter that had been Waugh's previous form of address. He had never overcome his opposition to her marriage to Frank and over the years had expressed his disapproval in various ways. After she became a Roman Catholic, Waugh's attitude underwent a complete change and he told Nancy Mitford a year later that 'Lady Pakenham is my great new friend'.

Elizabeth was grateful to Waugh for his biography of the

sixteenth-century Jesuit martyr *Edmund Campion* (1935), which had enabled her to bridge the gap separating intellect from feelings that was preventing her from feeling at home in the Catholic Church. In a letter to Evelyn Waugh (24th April 1946) she attempted to explain '. . . Your book gave me a thing I had been longing for for ages and thought I would never get – a really warm feeling for the Church and her heroes, comparable, I suppose, in strength to my logical conviction that she was right. I had told Gervase Mathew about this need of mine and he produced *Campion* for me. I felt quite different after reading it, though I could never explain how profoundly moved I was. Among other things it was the most tremendous relief and joy to find my whole self on the "right" side, the side I wanted to be on.'

But not all Elizabeth's friends were enthusiastic about her conversion; some, impugning her integrity, implied that she was merely pleasing Frank. There is no doubt that Frank played an important part in the decision, just as Elizabeth had been influential in his change of political allegiance; but the decision to become a Roman Catholic was very much her own, and although her views on church discipline may be less unyielding than the strict letter of Rome's law, her conduct, both public and private, is manifestly the fruit of committed belief.

8

A Political Family

Elizabeth was restless. She felt herself left behind while Frank was at the centre of affairs in Westminster. The Hopes, the Gordon Walkers and the Fawcetts had all left Oxford and gone to resume their peacetime lives in London. Despite her seven children, Elizabeth did not feel she had enough to do. She had considerable household help; in addition to Popey and her niece, May Munday, there was Liz Butler who came in every day, bringing her young daughter, Susan.

The extreme winter of 1946–7 did not help. This was to be the last winter at Chadlington Road, and it was one of the most severe on record, with prolonged snow, frost, fuel rationing and power cuts. The Pakenham children built an igloo in the garden, which survived from January to March. They welcomed the admonition from the Ministry of Fuel to cut down on washing![1] The continued austerity, with shortages and endless queues, contributed to the gloomy outlook. Rationing of clothes and sweets ended only in 1949, of petrol in 1950, of meat not until 1954. Popey never failed to produce family meals of some sort, most frequently a hotpot of root vegetables, and Elizabeth, overcoming her dislike of hens, always kept half a dozen, which helped to eke out the rations, but it was nevertheless a constant struggle to provide enough food to satisfy the tribe of growing children.

By the summer of 1946 the two eldest were at boarding-schools. Antonia, who was not yet fourteen, was taking School Certificate before moving from the Godolphin School in Salisbury to St Mary's, Ascot, where she was to be received into the Roman Catholic Church. Thomas was rising thirteen, but as he would one day receive an Irish title and property, it was decided to send him for one term to Belvedere, the Jesuit school in Dublin, where it was hoped that he would develop a sympathy for Ireland before going to Ampleforth, the Benedictine boarding-school in Yorkshire.

Paddy, aged nine, and Judith, six, were still at the Dragon, where Elizabeth continued to be fully involved in the life of the school. She agreed to present the prizes one year and her cherry-laden hat filled Paddy with embarrassment and shame. Four-year-old Rachel was in the nursery department of Greycote's School, where they all had started, and Michael and Catherine were too young for school.

There were now four girls and three boys. Catherine was eighteen months old and Elizabeth, although now forty-one, was beginning to experience the familiar yearning for a new baby; a fourth boy, she felt, would even up the sexes. The next baby was conceived in February 1947 during a rare night in London at the Dorchester which, even with post-war restrictions, provided a brief interlude of luxury away from the hurly-burly of Oxford.

The family were clearly outgrowing Chadlington Road and they would have to find a larger house. Elizabeth was increasingly tempted to leave Oxford and join her friends in London, but she found it hard to pull up Oxford roots and could not resist making an offer for Cumnor Manor, a Regency house south-west of Oxford. The offer was refused and Elizabeth finally decided in favour of Hampstead Garden Suburb, where she would be living not far from Evan Durbin, Hugh Gaitskell, Harold Wilson and Douglas Jay, the newly appointed Economic Secretary to the Treasury. The families were close and Elizabeth was assured of a warm welcome.

The Neo-Georgian six-bedroomed house at the end of Linnell Drive was more spacious than Chadlington Road and Elizabeth congratulated herself on finding a home that pleased everyone. She liked the large garden, Frank was delighted with the tennis court and children and staff benefited from an annexe that provided several extra rooms. A further advantage was that Hampstead was high enough to escape the suffocating smog that was an unpleasant and dangerous feature of London life until the Clean Air Act was enforced in 1956.

The age gap between fourteen-year-old Antonia and fifteen-month-old Catherine now made separate holidays for the teenagers essential. Elizabeth arranged for May, the nanny, to take Rachel, Michael and Catherine to lodgings in Bournemouth, while she took Antonia, Thomas, Paddy and Judith to Waterville in county Kerry for two weeks. Although Elizabeth was six months pregnant in August 1947 there was never any question of Frank's coming with her. Before the war, when Elizabeth had taken two or three children on holiday, he had occasionally joined them for a weekend, but sea, sand and swimming have never appealed to him.

The journeys to and from Ireland were made more disagreeable by an unreliable car and the overpowering stench on the ferry of Irish bullock, which a whole bottle of 'poppy scent', a present to Elizabeth from Thomas, did little to disguise. Paddy's principal memory of the Irish holiday is of his mother's spartan approach to swimming in the freezing sea. 'We won't bother to dry. Put your clothes on as you are and we'll go home.' On the other hand, Judith, who was seven at the time, has golden memories (as disclosed in an interview given to *Family Ties*, 1980). For the first time she was being grouped as one of the older ones, while at the same time, being the youngest in that group, was able to enjoy a privileged position. Hitherto, and sometimes afterwards, Judith felt that her mother resented her, the middle child, as the spearhead of the junior invaders, while she was caught fore and aft between mocking, indifferent elders and cheeky youngsters.

On 1st November 1947 Kevin was born in Linnell Drive – Elizabeth's addition to the post-war baby boom. His arrival had been preceded by that of sixteen-year-old Barbara Williamson to assist May in the nursery. Kevin was baptised at the local Catholic Church of St Edward the Confessor, his godparents including his sister Antonia and the painter Simon Elwes. After the baptism and without a word to Elizabeth, Simon seized the child and carried him off to the Lady altar, where he formally dedicated his new godson to Mary, the mother of God. Antonia, Thomas, Judith, Rachel and Michael had all been received into the Catholic Church, as had Catherine shortly after her birth.

The Pakenhams were now a Catholic family and attendance at Catholic schools was therefore becoming a priority. Antonia was at St Mary's, Ascot, and Thomas and Paddy were at Ampleforth. Judith, Rachel and Michael were sent to the Junior School of La Sagesse Convent in Golders Green.

Decisions were difficult. The privileged education that Thomas, Patrick, Michael and Kevin were to receive at Ampleforth flew in the face of the socialist principles of their parents. Frank and Elizabeth had endless arguments and discussions about education and were well aware of the paradox of their position. They concluded that it would be wrong to satisfy their consciences at the expense of the children and so the children were sent to private schools. Antonia has since observed that it would have been unrealistic, at that time and in that milieu, to expect her parents to consider anything but a fee-paying school and that they were to be commended for even considering an alternative to Eton.[2]

A major factor influencing the move to Hampstead had been the hope that Elizabeth would be able to see more of Frank, who had seldom been able to get back to Oxford during the week. In the autumn of 1946 Clement Attlee had reshuffled his Cabinet, offering Frank the position of Parliamentary

Secretary at the Ministry of National Insurance. Frank had not accepted the offer, but had instead asked for the post of Under-Secretary for War, which he had been given. In 1947 he left the War Office and was appointed Chancellor of the Duchy of Lancaster, with special responsibility for the British zones of Austria and Germany. This involved spending considerable time in Germany – he made twenty-six trips in twelve months. Elizabeth and Frank found the frequent partings hard, but that carried little weight compared with his anxiety at the results of the allied policy of destruction of German heavy industry. Frank and many others believed that the purpose of the dismantling policy was to wreak vengeance on the German people. Whatever the intention, the effect on Düsseldorf, in the British zone, had been to condemn the population to half starvation. Victor Gollancz reported in the *News Chronicle* that shortly after the war people in Düsseldorf were living on 400–1000 calories a day. Nazi regulations had specified 400–800 calories per day for the inmates of the Belsen concentration camp.

Frank opposed the policy both as a matter of Christian principle and because he was convinced that it would simply allow the Russians and their supporters to gain increasing influence, but in the climate of post-war Britain, his defence of the German people was unpopular. Elizabeth visited Bonn with him and was appalled by the suffering she saw. She gave full support to Frank's efforts to persuade Attlee and his Foreign Secretary, Ernest Bevin, to adopt a more humane policy. This was the first of several campaigns in which she was to back Frank's championship of an unpopular cause.

However, Frank's insistence on forgiveness for enemies extended beyond politics, and both he and Elizabeth were enthusiastic about employing German au pairs to help in the house and with the younger children. It was decreed that both Antonia and Thomas were to learn German, although Antonia was far from pleased by the decision. 'It was the most eccentric, horrifying idea at the time. People were so anti-German that they talked of killing dachshunds in the street. When I told Mother Hilda at St Mary's, Ascot, that I wanted to learn German, her native tongue, she cried with joy and said, "I never thought I would teach that language again".[3]

Ministerial office brought compensations as well as frustration and anxiety. In November 1947 the Pakenhams were in the front row of the central aisle at Westminster Abbey for the wedding of Princess Elizabeth to Lieutenant Philip Mountbatten. Elizabeth's only anxiety then was whether she could get through the crowds back to Hampstead in time for three-week-old Kevin's two-o'clock feed. She ran into a similar problem at a dinner given by the French ambassador in honour of Winston Churchill. The men remained so long over their port that the wives sent notes to ask them to rejoin the ladies. Clementine Churchill, however, was more direct. She confronted Winston in the dining room and told him that delay over the port was 'endangering the health of a nursing mother and her infant' (*The Pebbled Shore*, p. 257). This had an immediate effect, although Elizabeth did not reach Hampstead until 11.00 p.m., by which time Kevin was protesting loudly.

When the Pakenhams were invited to attend the state banquet in honour of Queen Juliana of The Netherlands on 21st November 1950, Elizabeth ran into further problems. She had combed the shops for the long white gloves demanded by Court etiquette and failing to find them had gone without; her bare arms displeased Queen Mary. Frank had made matters worse by genuflecting to George VI instead of bowing.

Later Elizabeth and Frank invited Clement Attlee and his wife, Violet, to dinner at Linnell Drive; in their honour Elizabeth decided to open the last bottle of the vintage port laid down by her grandfather, Arthur, the brother of Joseph Chamberlain. Elizabeth, Frank and the family were then invited to a Christmas party for the families of ministers, staff, tenants and friends given by the Attlees at Chequers, the Prime Minister's official country residence near Aylesbury. Gaitskells,

Durbins, Jays and Wilsons were also invited. There being so many guests coming from Hampstead, they travelled together in a hired bus, which, to everyone's embarrassment, arrived half an hour early, before Violet Attlee was ready for her guests.

On another occasion Elizabeth and Frank were invited to join the Attlees in a box at the opera with Ernest and Flo Bevin. Bevin was blatantly anti-German – 'I 'ates them' – and had bitterly opposed Frank over the dismantling of German industry. Intrigued, Elizabeth wished to get to know the Foreign Secretary better and hoped to sit beside him. She was mortified to find that wives were seated in the front of the box while husbands were left to slumber in the seats behind them. She had a similar disappointment at a dinner party in the Soviet Embassy, where she attempted to draw the Soviet statesman Vyacheslav Molotov into a discussion about the influence of Karl Marx on students. He pointedly switched the conversation by asking what she thought of the Georgian wine they were drinking.

In addition to official engagements Elizabeth had other occupations. In 1947 she had been appointed to the rent tribunal for the Paddington and St Pancras area. Rent tribunals were established by a Rent Control Act of 1946 covering properties in which rent included payment for services or furniture. The tribunals were set up by the Minister of Health in consultation with local authorities. Tenants could appeal to the tribunal, which had the power to approve, increase or lower rents. Elizabeth was known as an effective speaker and was sometimes asked to talk to informal groups on children or parenting. On one occasion when the Duke and Duchess of Windsor were on a private visit to London, Lord Dudley had arranged a dinner party for them at Claridges, to which he invited Elizabeth and Frank. Although Elizabeth was curious to meet the woman for whom Edward VIII had given up his throne, she was not prepared to cancel a lecture that she had agreed to give in the East End. Lord Dudley, determined that the two couples should meet, persuaded the Pakenhams to come on to Claridges as soon as Elizabeth's lecture was over. In her flat shoes and black jacket and skirt Elizabeth felt out of place among the diamonds and white ties. She was not impressed by the Duchess, who was wearing a black dress with sequins, 'which made her look like a shiny London lamppost on a rainswept night' (*The Pebbled Shore*, p. 266). Elizabeth found her easy to talk to, but she was really more interested in meeting the Duke than the Duchess.

In 1948, after a little more than a year as Chancellor of the Duchy of Lancaster with special responsibility for Germany and Austria, Frank was promoted to Minister of Civil Aviation. Within months of taking over the Ministry, a report commissioned by him, following a fatal accident, resulted in allegations of incompetence and calls for his resignation. Journalists staked out Linnell Drive and gave Elizabeth the first of many experiences of press hostility. Frank rode out the storm and survived in post.

In September 1948 Elizabeth and Frank were deeply grieved by a tragedy that saddened many of their circle. Evan Durbin was drowned while on holiday with his family in Cornwall. Evan, one of the leading Labour politicians of the day, had played a vital role in helping Frank to continue his political career after his defeat in 1945. He had given valuable advice to both Elizabeth and Frank, having been a close friend and colleague since undergraduate days.

The following year, 1949, Elizabeth was approached by the agent for the Oxford City Labour Party, who asked her to stand for the constituency in the general election that was expected shortly. This was a tempting offer; Frank's peerage now barred him from candidacy, and Elizabeth felt that the Party's invitation to her was an acknowledgment of Frank's work as their unsuccessful candidate in the 1945 election. The fact that her conversion to Roman Catholicism was not a barrier was, she felt, a tribute to them both. Frank had faced difficulties in 1940 when he had told his colleagues of his own conversion. Then the local party had insisted that he submit to a vote of confidence, which he had received without difficulty; and with the passage of time, he had regained respect. Elizabeth was pleased by this invitation to stand; being one of the few candidates who enjoyed canvassing, she had missed the excitement of the hustings. She was familiar with Oxford City constituency and well known and popular among the party workers.

One of the principal reasons for Elizabeth's resignation as Labour candidate for King's Norton in 1944 had been the fact that she had six children – she now had eight, although the older ones were becoming increasingly independent. Had she fought the King's Norton seat in 1945 there would have been every chance of victory, but five years on the country was tired of continuing restrictions and controls; disenchantment had set in and, as the Oxford City candidate, she could not expect to win. Paradoxically, this made the challenge more attractive to her. By accepting the invitation to stand, she could discharge what she perceived as her debt to the party. In large measure she owed her political awakening and much of the development of her confidence and skills to Ted Hobson, with whom she had lodged in Stoke-on-Trent; she was also indebted to Tom Baxter, her agent at King's Norton. The family were unlikely to be affected because victory was so improbable.

Elizabeth accepted the offer to stand and resolved to put everything she had into her campaign. In 1950 the contest would be markedly different from the 1945 Labour landslide. In Oxford City, constituency boundaries had at last been redrawn to include the working-class areas of Cowley and Headington, thereby greatly increasing the Labour vote. The campaign was generally good-tempered, although Elizabeth encountered criticism on account of the children. Judith, Rachel and Michael, aged respectively nine, seven and six, accompanied her, travelling back and forth from Hampstead to Oxford by coach each day. One anonymous letter-writer objected that the Pakenham children occupied bus seats, claiming that they were depriving those who could not afford a train fare. Another attacked Elizabeth for 'breeding like a rabbit'. A third detractor accused her of 'pure lust' – a splendid contradiction.

Elizabeth's campaign concentrated on Tory failure rather than on Labour policy. She castigated the Tories for their failure to tackle slum clearance, poverty and unemployment while in office. She claimed that they had betrayed the League of Nations and insisted that, as capitalists who upheld privilege, Tory proposals would damage the welfare state. She had the support of many undergraduates and a number of faculty members, including the future chairman of British Rail, Peter Parker, and her old friend and admirer Maurice Bowra. Frank, Hugh Gaitskell, Harold Wilson and John Parker, a future Lord Mayor of Oxford, all spoke on Elizabeth's behalf; she herself addressed each local trade union branch, holding a number of meetings at the factory gates. Although Elizabeth had banked on losing the election, she was nevertheless aware that her future turned on the outcome of the vote; active political life had always been and would remain an absorbing interest and she awaited the outcome with intense concern.

In 1945 Quintin Hogg had beaten Frank by 2800 and been returned as the Conservative member for Oxford City. Now, in 1950, he held the seat, beating Elizabeth with a majority of 3000. In his view[4] Elizabeth was 'a more formidable opponent' than Frank. He may have been right, but Elizabeth also had the newly drawn boundary in her favour, so her result was not particularly impressive. In 1950 Labour were returned to power but a national swing against the Government reduced their overall majority from 150 to three.

After the election Elizabeth took advantage of a warm spring day to visit Bernhurst, taking her mother and Michael with her. Her memories of happy school holidays and weekends in

Kent with her parents in their rented villa, Lynchfield, made her long for a country life for her own children. Furthermore, Linnell Drive was proving to be inconveniently far from the centre of London, specifically from the rent tribunal in Paddington or from social events, while the older children complained bitterly of the difficulties in meeting their friends.

Bernhurst was still a discouraging wreck. Where there had once been lawns, there were the concrete bases of Nissen huts. Weeds, brambles and abandoned barbed wire crowded out the few surviving rhododendrons and the three-hundred-year-old oak had lost most of its lower branches to the constant passage of lorries. The house had suffered less. Every surface had been painted a lurid yellow and the cellars were incurably damp as a result of the attempt by the Canadians to rig up showers and a laundry, but it was habitable and most of Great-Aunt Caroline's furniture was still in place. Elizabeth's inheritance from her father had been an unexpected windfall, but, with eight children to educate, the refurbishing of Bernhurst was out of the question. Nevertheless, Elizabeth and Frank felt that a move back to Sussex would be a considerable improvement on Hampstead Garden Suburb.

The family moved to Bernhurst on 30th July 1950, leaving Elizabeth little more than a month to search for new schools. This proved to be surprisingly easy, as Audrey Townsend, an old College friend, had set up Tates, a local junior school, which proved excellent for eight-year-old Rachel; Michael, who was seven, went to the village school, and three-year-old Catherine shared a governess with Susan Blinks, whose father was the local butcher. Kevin, aged two, was not yet old enough for formal lessons. Paddy was settled at Ampleforth, while Judith was miserably enduring Mayfield, a fashionable convent in Sussex. Thomas had just left Ampleforth, having won a classics exhibition to Oxford, while Antonia had arranged to leave St Mary's, Ascot, two years earlier without telling Elizabeth. 'What are your school sheets doing here?' her mother asked. 'I'm not going back next term,' said Antonia, who spent the next six months at the Lycée, before going to a crammer called Bendixens to be coached for the Oxford scholarship examinations. During this period Elizabeth had been preoccupied in establishing herself in London, giving lectures and supporting Frank in his ministerial duties and had left Antonia to organise her own life. This, she later acknowledged (writing in Antonia's record book) was a mistake. 'Judith shall not leave school at sixteen, we have learnt our lesson.'

Elizabeth has always shown unshakable confidence in Frank's ability. His success at the Ministry for Aviation was no surprise. There he converted the recently nationalised airlines, British European Airways and the British Overseas Airways Corporation, into profitable enterprises. In return he was hoping to be named Leader of the House of Lords, thus gaining the coveted Cabinet seat. Instead, in May 1951 Clement Attlee offered him the post of First Lord of the Admiralty, which then carried Cabinet rank and also gave him considerable influence in the Defence Committee of the Cabinet.[5] Moreover, Admiralty House, his official London residence off the Mall, was sufficiently large for ten Pakenhams. This change, coming so soon after the move to Bernhurst, was something of a mixed blessing and Admiralty House never became a family home: that role continued to be occupied by Bernhurst.

Just as the Admiralty appointment was announced Elizabeth again suffered a miscarriage. This time it nearly cost her her life. Most of the children were away at school, but Rachel arrived home to Bernhurst in time to watch, horror-struck, as her mother was carried into an ambulance on a stretcher. Although an injection restored Elizabeth to consciousness and saved her life, she was obliged to spend the next seven days in hospital. On her return she was greeted by Popey with, 'I never thought to see you again after you were carried out feet first.' Elizabeth very much wanted to give birth to another child, thereby expunging what seemed to her to be a negative conclusion to her childbearing years. However at forty-three the onset of the menopause ended any such hopes. She spent some weeks recovering at Bernhurst while Antonia, who was almost nineteen and had just completed her first year at Oxford, deputised for her mother at Admiralty House. This task was made easier by the naval personnel who provided the necessary domestic help.

Elizabeth recovered in time to accompany Frank on various official engagements. She dined with him on Nelson's flagship at Portsmouth and was struck by the smallness of HMS *Victory*. Clement Attlee, Lord and Lady Mountbatten, Hugh and Dora Gaitskell and the historian Sir Arthur Bryant were among the guests at official dinner parties; a cocktail party was also given at Admiralty House for Antonia and her friends. After the departure of the young guests, all the busts in the hall were found to have been livened up with lipstick!

Although bedrooms had been set aside in Admiralty House for the Pakenham children, these were hardly used. Antonia spent the summer of 1951 there and Kevin and Catherine stayed for a few days' holiday with their nanny, Barbara, who had taken charge of the nursery after May left to be married. Elizabeth arranged that the children's visit should coincide with Trooping the Colour, which they watched from Admiralty House. She also organised visits to Battersea funfair and the waxworks at Madame Tussauds.

In the event Frank was to spend only a few months at the Admiralty. In October 1951 the Labour Government lost their tiny majority and went out of office. Frank lost his job and, unlike his friends in the House of Commons, lost his salary too.[6] Without too much difficulty he was able to return to teaching politics part-time at Christ Church, but he would now have the inconvenience of travelling to the House of Lords from either Oxford or Bernhurst. Elizabeth also had to commute from Bernhurst for her work on the rent tribunal. A house in London seemed essential and, with Frank teaching again, it was financially possible to consider a London base in addition to Bernhurst, which could still be used for weekends and holidays.

9

Impending Tragedy

At the end of the summer of 1952 Elizabeth established her family at 14 Cheyne Gardens in Chelsea, an area that had always fascinated her on account of the historical associations with Henry VIII and Thomas More. This was her sixth move during her twenty-one years of marriage and she had learnt from previous mistakes. The three-storeyed Victorian house was five minutes' walk from the fashionable King's Road and had access to good public transport. Cheyne Gardens was also near to the Albert Bridge and the most direct route south to Bernhurst. Now that Elizabeth was based in London, the schools problem for the five younger children was quickly resolved.

Judith was removed from Mayfield and sent to More House, a new Catholic day school run by the canonesses of St Augustine in Cromwell Road; Michael went to St Philip's preparatory school in Kensington in preparation for Ampleforth. Rachel, Catherine and Kevin were taken to the Holy Child Convent in Cavendish Square, near Oxford Circus, by Barbara, their nanny. For Kevin, who was not yet five, the long journey across London proved overtiring; he forgot what he had known and learnt nothing new. Elizabeth therefore decided to teach him herself, relying on guidelines issued by the Parents National Educational Union. She organised a full curriculum and gained grudging acceptance of her teaching from the schools inspector who came to Cheyne Gardens to check on the child's progress.

Elizabeth enjoyed teaching Kevin, but was less enthusiastic about the work of the committees that she was asked to join. She was already serving on a rent tribunal and was now asked to sit on a youth commission for the Labour Party as well as a maternity and allied services committee set up by the Ministry of Health. A third, rather different committee was that of the Catholic Library, which was in the process of transferring to new premises. Frank's friend David Astor, the owner of the *Observer*, asked Elizabeth to join the committee of the Africa Bureau, which he had recently set up to support African leaders in the British territories that were striving for autonomy. Members of the committee were mostly intellectuals or Establishment figures. Despite her dislike of committee work, Elizabeth found herself in sympathy with the work of the Bureau. She also became increasingly curious about the activities undertaken by her uncle Joseph Chamberlain at the end of the nineteenth century, when he served as Colonial Secretary in Lord Salisbury's government.

As her public work increased Elizabeth also began to gain a reputation as a broadcaster. She was invited to join the popular BBC *Brains Trust*, but her service on the panel was cut short. The members were asked what they believed to be the purpose of life. '*Ad majorem Dei gloriam* [to the greater glory of God],' replied Elizabeth. She was to learn later that Julian Huxley, the well-known scientist and fellow panel member, was chiefly responsible for her dismissal. He considered that the reputation for enlightenment that the *Brains Trust* was trying to present was damaged by the introduction of God into an answer.

Elizabeth and Frank also enjoyed a busy social life. Although Frank was no longer a member of the government, as a peer he was invited with his wife to the coronation of Elizabeth II. Frank's uncle Lord Dunsany offered to take them with him to the Abbey in his chauffeur-driven car, which to Elizabeth's alarm started heading in the wrong direction. 'It transpired that his coronet had been left behind in Ireland and he was looking for the house of an absent nobleman of the same rank as himself' (*The Pebbled Shore*, p. 285; a similar story, referring to the coronation of George V, appears in Mark Amory's biography of Lord Dunsany (1972), p. 80). Once the house had been found he had only to persuade the valet to part with his employer's coronet for the day.

A custom introduced after the accession of Elizabeth II was that of holding small dinner parties to enable the Queen and Prince Philip to meet 'interesting people' from all walks of life. Elizabeth and Frank were invited to one of these dinners, at which the Queen amused her guests with an account of her ordeal at the hands of the BBC's make-up department in preparation for her televised Christmas message: '. . . The first time my white skin and broad jaw made my face come out like a huge, white plate with two dark cavities containing black boot buttons . . .' Later on Elizabeth and Frank were again guests at the Palace for the more formal state banquet held in honour of President Heuss of West Germany.

Having four daughters and four sons, Elizabeth was increasingly regarded as an expert on the upbringing of children. She was often asked to advise journalists, until Eve Perrick of the *Daily Express*, believing that Elizabeth should have the credit, arranged a meeting with Anthony Hern, the features editor, to explore the possibility of commissioning Elizabeth to write articles herself. Anthony gave her helpful advice and Elizabeth submitted a piece called 'What do we learn from fantasy?', which was approved by Max Beaverbrook, the proprietor of the paper.[1] He agreed to give her a weekly column and also invited Elizabeth and Frank to Cherkley, his country house in Surrey. She drove back to Bernhurst well satisfied with the weekend. On hearing that her children were always hungry, Beaverbrook had told his footman to fill Elizabeth's car boot with tins of food, part of his wartime reserve, which had remained hidden away behind bookshelves. She had also secured a job on the paper.

In her weekly articles Elizabeth touched on many issues, from adventure to delinquency and make-believe to meals. She knew only too well how easily family meals could degenerate into drawn-out squabbles over food. Charles Anson, a friend of Michael and the Queen's future press secretary, likened meals at Bernhurst to the scrimmage of animals feeding in a David Attenborough film. There was never enough for all the children to have a second helping; Michael even suggested that they write a book on their childhood entitled *Look Back in Hunger*.

Jealousy was another issue with which Elizabeth dealt, again drawing on her experience with her own children. She referred for example to a bitter family row caused by Judith's refusal to allow Rachel to wear a favourite frock that she had outgrown, declaring that she would rather have it burnt. Many of Elizabeth's articles referred to discipline and specifically to corporal punishment, to which she was strongly opposed, although in the early days she had sometimes been driven to spank the older ones. Elizabeth described alternative methods of punishment, which she had found to be effective with her own younger children.

Anthony Hern had warned Elizabeth of the difficulties of introducing religion, and she generally avoided the subject. Unlike her mother, she had preferred to leave religious teaching to nannies; even after her conversion to Catholicism she had been unsuccessful in her attempt to introduce family prayers at the end of the day. In 1951, influenced by the campaign of an American Catholic priest, Father Patrick Paton, she had tried to introduce the saying of the family rosary.[2] The children, then ranging in age from eighteen (Antonia) to three (Kevin), refused to be serious; they were so rowdy and argumentative that Elizabeth gave up after the second attempt.

In 1954 a collection of Elizabeth's articles on children was published by Weidenfeld and Nicolson under the title *Points for Parents*. This modest book hardly lived up to what might have been expected of the 'Isis Idol' of 1930, but it had gained Elizabeth a publisher, establishing a strong position for further work. George Weidenfeld had arrived in England before the war as a penniless refugee from Austria, and had later met Frank in Oxford. He had set up a successful and expanding publishing house and in 1953 was looking for promising and intelligent young women with a flair for editing. He turned to Frank, who suggested Antonia. She was then almost twenty-one, had just taken her degree in history and was described by George as 'good-looking, very intelligent, with a mixture of modesty and self-confidence'. George employed Antonia and consequently met her mother.

George Weidenfeld was immediately captivated by Elizabeth and determined that she should become one of his authors. He believed that the public's interest in children, coupled with Elizabeth's experience in dealing with them, would result in a series of books that could be expanded year by year. When it became clear that there was no market for such a series, he suggested that she edit a symposium by prominent Roman Catholics on the teaching of the Church. The idea appealed to Elizabeth who approached possible contributors. Evelyn Waugh turned her down, deriding the £25 fee, but others agreed to write for her, including Fr Martin D'Arcy, Douglas Woodruff and Frank. *Catholic Approaches* was published by Weidenfeld and Nicolson in 1955, arousing limited interest, although it was later taken up by the Catholic Book Club.

Elizabeth could hope that after her second book other commissions would follow, especially as she was by then contributing to Catholic journals including *The Tablet* and *The Universe.* In 1960 when her column on the *Daily Express* came to an end, she moved on to the *News of the World* and later in 1960 to the *Sunday Times.* Lord Beaverbrook had warned her that once she began to write for the newspapers there would be no escape, a situation that suited Elizabeth. Her earnings were a helpful supplement to the family budget, which, with a second house to run, was increasingly difficult to manage.

Fortunately Elizabeth had been well trained in thrift during her youth. Forgetful of her own struggles with her father, whom she was unable to persuade to leave lights burning, she was no less ruthless in turning off lights and electric fires. She believed that it did her children no harm to wash in cold water, share crowded bedrooms, wear passed-down clothes and eat simply, such treats as orange squash being reserved for Sundays.

Elizabeth herself always enjoys a fine meal if one is put before her, but of all common occupations she is least interested in eating. She actively dislikes cooking and successfully avoided doing it for sixty years. When Popey finally retired in 1954 a satisfactory replacement proved so difficult to find that Elizabeth engaged an Icelandic au pair, Kirstie. Before Kirstie arrived, with Karl, her mentally handicapped small boy, Elizabeth consulted her own children about taking Karl in. For once the children were agreed. 'Over our dead bodies,' they said. 'Bad luck,' said Elizabeth. 'I've employed his mother and of course she must bring her child with her.' It must be said that the children were objecting on the grounds of space rather than the child's disability.

Additionally Elizabeth had various part-time helpers for the children. She was therefore comparatively free of domestic responsibilities and in 1955, when the printers' strike halted the publication of newspapers, she was temporarily released from her column as well. Taking Paddy with her, she joined a party of friends for a cultural Greek cruise on board the S S *Aigaion*. On the same ship was her old flame Maurice Bowra, the Dominican Fr Gervase Mathew, who had instructed her ten years earlier, her friends Sheila Birkenhead and Pam Berry, and their sons who made a trio with Paddy. He was now eighteen, had left Ampleforth and was waiting to take up the classical scholarship that he had won at Magdalen College, Oxford. By day there were visits to places of interest while in the evenings Gervase Mathew, Mortimer Wheeler and Maurice

Bowra gave relevant lectures. Elizabeth, in her element, was fired with the desire to undertake some serious historical writing herself, a desire that later bore fruit in *Jameson's Raid*, her first historical work.

Preparations for Antonia's wedding to Hugh Fraser, however, cut across all attempts at regular work.[3] Hugh, a Roman Catholic and a Conservative, was a younger son of the fourteenth Lord Lovat; he was fourteen years older than Antonia and had been known to Elizabeth and Frank since shortly before the outbreak of the Second World War. Over six foot tall, Hugh had been a strikingly obvious figure leading an antiappeasement student march in Oxford in 1938. The marriage of the eldest daughter of a prominent peer to a Member of Parliament was a society event and for all her poise Antonia, who was then almost twenty-four, became increasingly tense. Some weeks before the wedding Elizabeth took Antonia shopping for a dress for herself. The first one she tried was perfect but cost £20, and Elizabeth turned it down in favour of another that was half the price and, to Antonia, half as pretty. 'Why?' she demanded, almost in tears. 'Because,' said Elizabeth firmly, 'I promised myself that I would give the same sum to charity that I spent on the dress, and I can't afford £20.' 'This is my wedding, not your good deed,' Antonia blazed at her mother, but Elizabeth was not to be moved.

Antonia and Hugh were married in the Roman Catholic Church of the Assumption in Warwick Street on 25th September 1956 and a reception was held in the Fishmongers' Hall. Emerging from the church to the sound of bagpipes, they were a fine romantic pair. Antonia wore a Mary Queen of Scots cap, Hugh was in a kilt and had a *sgian dubh* (black knife) in his stocking. Even Elizabeth, normally so calm and controlled, was tearful. 'I wept on Antonia's wedding day, something I didn't do at the weddings of any of my other children, it was such a huge thing to be losing her from the family.' The 'loss' would shortly be compensated. Within weeks Antonia was expecting a child.

Soon after, on 3rd November 1956, Elizabeth and Frank celebrated their own silver wedding with a party at Cheyne Gardens. Quintin Hogg arrived half an hour early and left almost immediately, before any other guests arrived. As First Lord of the Admiralty under Anthony Eden he was preoccupied with the Suez crisis provoked by Nasser's successful bid to assume control of the Canal.[4] Pacing up and down the Pakenhams' drawing room, full of anxiety for 'his' ships sailing for Egypt, he was in no mood for celebrations.

During the 1950s Elizabeth's concerns were not wholly centred on family affairs; she and Frank were much occupied with efforts to provide a Catholic church in their own village of Hurst Green. For many years Sunday mass had been said alternately in the Hurst Green Memorial Hall or in the upper room of The Rose and Crown, a public house in the neighbouring village of Burwash. Local Catholics approached the Longfords, asking for a gift of land on which a church could be built. Elizabeth agreed that Frank should hand over one of the Bernhurst fields and the task of raising funds to build the church began. After several years of fêtes, bazaars, raffles and jumble sales, the Church of Our Lady Help of Christians was finally built, to the design of the architect Francis Pollen, the son of an old friend. He erected a semicircular building, designing and commissioning pews with which to furnish it. These were 'specially imported from Ireland for our discomfort,' Elizabeth told the author, sotto voce, as they attended mass together.

Meanwhile Elizabeth was President of the London Writers' Circle, Life President of the Society of Women Writers and Journalists, and a member both of the St Joan's Alliance – a small Roman Catholic feminist society – and of the Fawcett Society.

Given her determination that husband and children should be no bar to a career, Elizabeth might seem to be a model feminist, although her moderation fails to find favour with radicals. As an undergraduate she had insisted on signing the visitors' book after dining at Christ Church. She had pursued a career for the first twelve years of her marriage, and in her late eighties, in 1994, joined CWO, Catholic Women for Ordination. She has never doubted that girls are the 'top sex', claiming that they have special powers of concentration, attention to detail, understanding, creativity and instinct for preservation. She believes that these gifts develop as a result of '. . . patiently carrying a child for nine months [and] protecting, loving it and teaching it'.[5] She believes passionately that women should be in charge of their own fertility. 'Choice not chance' expresses her view, which has led to open disagreement with the Church's teaching on birth control.[6]

Elizabeth is no extremist. Much as she prized a 'full life', when in 1944 her career appeared to conflict with the needs of Frank and the children, she gave it up, fully aware that her resignation would end her chances of an active political career. She respects women who are content to make care for their families their career and has no sympathy for the view that men and women are the same. She supports the ordination of women to the Catholic priesthood, but is opposed to changing the Scriptures in order to achieve 'inclusive language'.[7]

By the time Elizabeth reached her fiftieth birthday in 1956, her views had taken root. By then she was aware of so many blessings that she had a niggling anxiety that the gods had been overgenerous and had some disaster in store. In 1954 Frank had abandoned teaching to take up the chairmanship of the National Bank, a post he was to hold with success for the next nine years. She was the mother of eight healthy, intelligent children for whom she had been able to provide the best private education. Antonia, married to an up-and-coming Member of Parliament, had produced Rebecca, the first grandchild, thrilling Elizabeth by inviting her to be present at her birth. She lived a busy life with her various committees and friends, among whom she was much in demand. Many social functions took place in London, but from 1950 Sussex was her refuge. At Bernhurst she could indulge her passion for gardening and exchange visits with a circle of friends. Chief among these were Kitty and Malcolm Muggeridge, old friends and neighbours with whom she and Frank had a great deal in common.

Elizabeth enjoyed a good life, but was it really the 'full life' to which she had always aspired? What had happened to the radical who had met the hunger marchers in Cambridge, or been thrown out of the Labour Party for following her own line in King's Norton? Might not her life since then be regarded as representing an abandonment of earlier principles?

Her foothold in the world of journalism could hardly be called a career and there seemed little likelihood that it would become one. But it was just at this time that she was becoming interested in the Jameson Raid, Dr Leander Starr Jameson's plans for a raid against the South African Republic, and the degree to which her great-uncle Joseph Chamberlain had been implicated. Her investigations were to take four years, a crucial period in which she acquired the skills of a serious historian. The resulting book, *Jameson's Raid*, and all her subsequent works are discussed in a later chapter.

Every summer Elizabeth had taken the children on holiday, even braving the difficulties of war. Once while she was nursing Judith in 1941 they had undertaken an eight-hour journey to Cornwall. But just as her parents had been loth to go away once they had established themselves at Lynchfield, so after 1950 Elizabeth was loth to leave Bernhurst and all the work of the garden. However, in 1959 Catherine suggested to her mother that she ought to give them cultural holidays. Elizabeth took the bait and decided on a tour of Wales, with Rachel, aged sixteen, Michael, fifteen, and Catherine, thirteen. Eleven-year-old Kevin stayed meanwhile with a schoolfriend. Elizabeth allowed the teenagers to choose the places to be visited. The highlight was their visit to Tintern Abbey in the Wye valley. Huddled under an umbrella, they listened in rapt silence to

Rachel reading *Lines Written a Few Miles above Tintern Abbey* by William Wordsworth; Elizabeth had had the foresight to bring his collected works with her.

Wales was so successful that in the following year Elizabeth embarked on a more ambitious programme, taking Kevin with them this time. Driving north, they saw the Cotswolds, Stratford on Avon, the Lake District, Hadrian's Wall and the Borders. On the return journey they visited Yorkshire, Lincolnshire and Cambridgeshire.

This holiday coincided with a brief break between books. *Jameson's Raid* had been published in the spring of 1960, before Elizabeth embarked on her biography of Queen Victoria. Knowing how close her mother had been to Joe Chamberlain, Elizabeth was concerned that criticism of him would prove hurtful. She need not have worried. Mrs Harman read and thoroughly enjoyed her daughter's book, which she lived just long enough to see published; Katherine Harman died on 10th June 1960, aged eighty-seven. She had outlived her husband by fifteen years and had known two of her greatgrandchildren, Antonia's daughters, Rebecca and Flora. Elizabeth had always been close to her mother and she grieved for her loss.

Early in 1961 the childless Edward, the sixth Earl of Longford, suffered a sudden stroke and died soon after. He was then fifty-eight. Frank, who was three years younger, succeeded him as the seventh Earl, but by a previous arrangement Thomas, a bachelor of twenty-seven, inherited Pakenham Hall, which he restored to its ancient name of Tullynally. The death of Edward brought virtually no change to Frank and Elizabeth's position, since, apart from the family titles, the whole inheritance had been passed to Thomas.

Frank, still hankering after a career in the Commons, consulted his old friend Hugh Gaitskell who was now leader of the Labour Party. Frank wanted to explore the possibility of renouncing the hereditary seat in the House of Lords that he had inherited from Edward and also the peerage of Baron

Pakenham of Cowley granted in 1945.[8] Gaitskell made no promises but in the summer of 1962 Frank felt sufficiently confident of entering the Commons to announce that he intended to resign his chairmanship of the National Bank in the following year. He needed to give himself time to look for a constituency that he could represent at the next general election.

Gaitskell could not be of any assistance. To the great loss of the Labour Party, he died of a chest infection in January 1963 at the age of fifty-six. For Elizabeth and Frank, his death was not only the cause of deep personal sorrow but the end of whatever chance there might have been of a Commons career for Frank. Harold Wilson, Gaitskell's successor, was to lead the Labour Party to a paper-thin majority of five seats in the election of 1964. The new Labour leader had no comparable friendship or affinity with Frank, nor any desire to see him in the Commons; the Peerages Renunciation Bill was already contentious and Wilson did not want to press Harold Macmillan's government for additional amendments. After his election victory, however, Wilson did appoint Frank as Leader of the House of Lords, which gave him a much coveted seat in the Cabinet.

Elizabeth was greatly cheered by Frank's promotion, which came the year after a harrowing accident. In the summer of 1963 Paddy had taken two of his friends sailing; his boat turned turtle and Paddy, after being in the water for eighteen hours, undertook a two-hour swim to reach the shore and summon help. This arrived too late to save his friends David Winn and Sarah d'Avigdor Goldsmid, the daughter of Elizabeth's old friend Harry. The coroner ruled that both had died by mis-adventure, praising the fight that they had all put up to stay alive. Nevertheless, Elizabeth was deeply distressed by the tragedy.

Apart from this, the 1960s were generally a time of celebra-tion, with several family weddings. Elizabeth was pleased to see her children becoming settled, and delighted in the lessening of her own immediate responsibilities. In 1963 Judith, who was active in the Labour Party, married Alec Kazantzis, another party member. In the following year the eldest son, Thomas, who was living at Pakenham, now renamed Tullynally, married Valerie McNair Scott. This was a particular joy for Elizabeth and Frank because Valerie was the niece of two of their oldest friends, Sheila Birkenhead and Michael Berry.[9]

Her new daughter-in-law endeared herself to Elizabeth by her strong desire to live at Tullynally, which remained one of Elizabeth's favourite places for holidays. In 1964 Elizabeth had completed her biography of Queen Victoria and was about to begin on one of Wellington. She was therefore thankful to be able to send Kevin and Catherine, then sixteen and seventeen, to Thomas and Valerie shortly after their marriage, which enabled her to get on with her writing in peace. Elizabeth herself came for the odd weekend. Fortunately Valerie enjoyed a full house, although she was somewhat overwhelmed coming back to Tullynally after her honeymoon to find there 'an enormous crowd of Pakenhams sitting round the table eating their heads off and apparently staying forever.'[10]

It was also in 1964 that Elizabeth was asked by Dr Helen Gardner, a Fellow of St Hilda's College, Oxford, if she would allow her name to go forward for the post of principal of the College. Elizabeth found this offer tempting. She loved Oxford, she has always been attracted to young people, especially to young intellectuals and from the point of view of her children the timing was perfect. Seventeen-year-old Kevin, her youngest, was then in his final year at Ampleforth and she and Frank had recently moved from Cheyne Gardens to a two-bedroomed apartment in a modern block of flats, Chesil Court, near by. On the other hand, there were difficulties to overcome. Frank, kept in London by his ministerial responsibilities, would have to spend the week there on his own. Elizabeth's memories of wartime travel had left her with a dread of long, cross-country journeys such as Bernhurst to Oxford. If she accepted the Oxford appointment she would be making this journey twice a week during term-time. Elizabeth also had to take into account the official entertaining that she would have to undertake as the wife of a minister. The balance was finally tipped by her writing. Elizabeth had already embarked on the biography of Wellington and was not prepared to disrupt the agreed schedule; she therefore explained to Dr Gardner that she could not let her name go forward. This decision was hers alone; Frank had not tried to influence her, having promised his full support whatever she decided.

Towards the end of 1964, however, Elizabeth did agree to a brief interruption of her work. She accepted an invitation to visit the United States as the guest of the city fathers and mothers of New Orleans. The original invitation came to Frank, but as the celebrations concerned the 150th anniversary of the defeat of the British at New Orleans, he found himself 'not free' to leave England. In 1815 General Edward Pakenham had been soundly defeated and killed by the Americans, led by General Andrew Jackson. Invitations were sent to the two generals' senior surviving descendants. As a minister of Her Majesty's Government, Frank could hardly accept an invitation commemorating a British defeat, so he was represented by Elizabeth, Thomas and Valerie; as Michael was then completing a post graduate course at Rice University in Texas, he too joined his family at New Orleans.

The eight-day visit, Elizabeth's first experience of the United States, was a great success; Elizabeth helped to plant commemorative oaks, watched a *son et lumière* in New Orleans's Jackson Square and danced at a Victory Ball. Finally, exhausted, she was thankful to get away for a brief holiday with Anne and Christopher Fremantle, former Oxford friends, who were then at Acapulco, Mexico. Elizabeth was fascinated by the pre-Columbian pyramids which Thomas declared to be finer than anything in Egypt apart from the Sphinx. She swam in a small bay near Acapulco, where an encounter with a large snake left her unharmed and added to her sense of adventure.

Elizabeth enjoyed this visit to the United States as she did all official functions in which she was included as the wife of a government minister. Shortly after her return to England, she accompanied Frank to St Paul's Cathedral for Winston Churchill's funeral. A few months later in June 1965 she was with him again on a visit to Belgium for the 150th anniversary of the Battle of Waterloo. They flew to Brussels, lunched with the Ambassador and the Duke and Duchess of Kent and then went on to the drumhead service at Hougoumont.[11] During the review the rain poured down, just as it had done on the day of the battle. On both occasions the white belts of the soldiers were stained red; what Elizabeth saw was no more than dye that had run off the ceremonial coats – in Wellington's day, the white belts were stained with blood.

Soon after her return from Belgium Elizabeth began work on her biography of Wellington; this was to take eight years to complete. She could concentrate on her own research in the knowledge that Frank was fully occupied with his new post. As the result of a reshuffle, Wilson had added to Frank's responsibilities in the Lords by appointing him Secretary of State for the Colonies. Three years later, in 1967, Rachel married the film director Kevin Billington and the following year Paddy married Mary Plummer.

To Elizabeth's great satisfaction, several of the children were establishing themselves as writers and meriting headlines such as 'Ladies in Writing' or 'Ink in the Blood'. In 1968 Michael wrote from the British Embassy in Warsaw, where he was Second Secretary, '. . . every time I open a paper I see a member of the family smiling out of it. Are you all using the same press agent or is there an entire firm under contract?' In 1969 Christina Foyle, daughter of the founder of Foyle's bookshop in Charing Cross Road, gave one of her famous monthly luncheons for authors and their readers at the Dorchester Hotel in honour of all the 'literary Longfords', giving rise to a press report headed 'One family, seven writers, twenty books'.

But although the children were excelling themselves, Frank's active political career was ending. In January 1968, when he was sixty-four, he resigned from the government on a question of principle. The 1966 Labour manifesto had pledged to raise the school-leaving age, but the deepening financial crisis of 1967 led Harold Wilson to propose a number of savings including deferment of the promised educational reform. Frank was not prepared to accept this. His resignation saddened Elizabeth; they had both enjoyed his political life, and she would miss it almost as much as he.

By this time Elizabeth was half-way through her biography of the Duke of Wellington. She had completed the first volume, which took Wellington to the victory of Waterloo, and before starting the second volume she planned a break, taking Rachel with her to visit Michael and her old friend Nicko Henderson, who was then the British Ambassador in Warsaw. The holiday had to be postponed on account of work on the Wellington proofs, but she finally left for Poland in August 1969. By then Elizabeth was ready for a holiday; the previous months had been hectic; while she was correcting the proofs twenty-three-year-old Catherine had moved temporarily into the flat. At this time Elizabeth's youngest daughter was working on the *Sunday Telegraph* and, having lost the flat she shared with a friend, had been taken in by her parents. Catherine was the most rebellious of the children; she was argumentative and frequently challenged her father's views. The flat was too small for three adults, and Elizabeth had found Catherine's friends, her untidy clutter and noise a nearly intolerable invasion of her working space. For the first and only time, Elizabeth left the country without first speaking to Catherine on the telephone though she knew, of course, Catherine's weekend plans.

She had not been away long before tragedy struck. On 12th August, after a gloomy day spent visiting Hitler's wartime headquarters at Rastenburg, they returned to their hotel at Gdansk to find a message asking them to contact Frank urgently. When Michael 'phoned he was told by his father that Catherine had been killed in a car crash early that morning with her two friends Gina Richardson and Stefan Tyszko. The young people had been spending the weekend in Suffolk and were returning to work early on Monday morning. Catherine was asleep on the back seat when the driver overtook on a blind corner and crashed headlong into a lorry.

Elizabeth's one thought was to get back to Frank. Her loss was beyond comfort, and separation from him was unbearable. If only she had not gone to Poland Catherine would have been safe with her at Bernhurst and she would still be alive. Catherine was identified by Frank, and her requiem was held at the church of Our Most Holy Redeemer and St Thomas More, Chelsea, where Elizabeth regularly attends mass; later the body was cremated. The church was full and many of the congregation went on to a wake held at Antonia and Hugh's home in Campden Hill Square.

Gradually, haltingly, Elizabeth's faith made the loss more bearable, preventing her from asking 'why me?' – a question that implied, in Elizabeth's view, that it was all right for someone else's daughter to die but not hers. In time she was to find comfort in praying each day for Catherine and her friends and in the growing certainty that Catherine was 'all right'.

Fr Martin D'Arcy came to Bernhurst for a night. He talked about the doctrine of purgatory, helping Elizabeth to understand and even to find comfort in a doctrine that she had previously found distressing. Dante's *Purgatorio* and Thomas More's last letter to his daughter – 'Pray for me, and I shall pray for you and all your friends, that we may merrily meet in Heaven' – gradually penetrated Elizabeth's desolation. She began to find some consolation in memories. She recalled the

Elizabeth Longford

time that one of Catherine's contemporaries had died; 'I don't think it's sad to die young,' she had said then. At Easter, just a few months earlier, Catherine had been to Jerusalem and there, uncharacteristically, had gone to confession and communion. 'Well, you never know what's going to happen!' she had said, in response to her mother's surprise.

The memorials also brought some comfort. A tablet was placed in the Hurst Green church, a summer house in the garden and a seat by the front gate. This was in joint memory of Catherine and two of her contemporaries from Hurst Green who had died the same year: Susan Blinks, who had shared a governess with Catherine, died of cancer; and Billy Oakley was killed in a train crash.

Elizabeth has found that involvement with the Catherine Pakenham Memorial Award, which she and Frank set up, has been a long-term consolation and a means of helping her to think of her daughter in a positive way. The *Daily Telegraph* contributed to the capital needed for the award, which is open to women aged between eighteen and twenty-five. Entrants are asked to submit a non-fiction article of between 750 and 2000 words on any subject. The winner receives £1000. Elizabeth chaired the panel of judges until 1980, when her third daughter Rachel took over the task. Most of the winners have gone on to make a career in journalism: they have included Polly Toynbee, Tina Brown, Sally Beauman and Valerie Grove.

Elizabeth was surprised by the abyss of mourning into which she was plunged by the death of Catherine, although gradually she began to realise that she was probably grieving more for her own sense of diminishment than for the loss of her daughter. Grief, with its debilitating pain, became less acute with the passage of time, although she would never be free of her 'unending sense of loss' (*Diary*, 11th August 1990). But there was solace to be found in writing. The biography of the Duke of Wellington was only half finished. *Wellington: The Years of the*

138

Sword, which ended with the Battle of Waterloo in 1815, was topping the bestseller lists, although Wellington's political life awaited completion.

10

'Early Afternoon'

On Elizabeth's sixtieth birthday, in 1966, Paddy made a speech in which he described his mother as entering upon the evening of her life. 'Not evening, early afternoon,' Elizabeth rapidly corrected. She had by then made a name for herself with her biography of Queen Victoria; she would continue to write, producing another seven biographies, two anthologies, several books connected with the royal family and her own memoirs. The concentrated work that this was to entail made a vivid contrast with what she had expected of her later years: she had foreseen a leisured life, picturing herself relaxing in the garden with a book or embroidery (interview with Eileen Ashcroft, *Evening Standard,* 1956).

In 1964 Elizabeth was appointed a trustee of the National Portrait Gallery, where she was also a member of the sub-committee for portraits of the living. The director (1967–73), Roy Strong, valued her contribution. He recalls an occasion when her common sense brought her colleagues to order. He wanted to redecorate the gallery; most of the trustees believed that this should be their, not the Director's, responsibility. 'If this gallery is redecorated by the people sitting at this table, it will be redecorated according to the lowest common denominator,' Elizabeth said, settling the matter. Elizabeth's original term of office was extended and when she finally retired from the board in 1978 several members regretted that she could not serve for a third term. She had by then served for six years (1969–75) on the Advisory Committee of the Victoria and Albert Museum, and was still (1976–80) on the Advisory Board of The British Library.

Elizabeth's social life also continued to expand. In the early 1970s she met Margaret and Dennis Thatcher at a dinner party given by Thelma Cazalet in her flat in Scotney Castle in Kent. The Thatchers then had a house at Lamberhurst, a few miles from Bernhurst. Elizabeth invited them to dinner but this was not a great success, as Elizabeth has always had mixed feelings towards the future Prime Minister. Some members of her family put Elizabeth's ambivalence down to feelings of rivalry or even jealousy. In 1979, shortly after Margaret Thatcher gained the leadership of the Conservative Party, Elizabeth was asked what she felt about the country being led by a woman. 'If only it did not have to be *that* woman,' she had replied gloomily (*Diary* entry), having always wanted Shirley Williams to be the first woman premier.

Elizabeth was no longer in the political arena, but she was making her name in literary circles. Her biography of Queen Victoria won the James Tait Black prize in 1964. *Wellington: The Years of the Sword*, her first volume on the Duke, was chosen by the *Yorkshire Post* as their Best Book of the Year for 1969. The following year she was elected a Fellow of the Royal Society of Literature and Sussex University conferred on her an honorary doctorate in literature. Not long after, in the New Year's Honours List for 1974, she was appointed a Commander of the Order of the British Empire.

At this time, Frank was receiving a particularly bad press. He had begun his campaign against pornography in 1971 and was immediately dubbed 'Lord Porn'. At first Elizabeth was opposed to Frank's involvement; as a writer, she was against any form of censorship, but she changed her mind when she began to learn of the extent of pornography and its effects, especially on young children. 'I had never thought about pornography before and I was really shocked,' she said in an interview with *News of the World*.[1] She was appalled to learn that one particularly disturbing magazine was found in the desk of a fourteen-year-old child.

In 1971 after making an impassioned speech in the House of Lords, Frank set up a private commission of enquiry and spent a weekend in Denmark, where hardcore pornography was freely available. In the past, Elizabeth had criticised Frank for attacking subjects about which he knew little; he was determined that this time no one would be able to accuse him of ignorance. Going against well-informed advice, he courted publicity during his enquiries and even invited the press to accompany him to Denmark; as a result, he and his serious intent were nationally ridiculed.

The hostile publicity engendered by the anti-pornography campaign had not died down when Frank made himself even more unpopular by becoming Myra Hindley's champion. She was Ian Brady's lover and accomplice in the notorious 'Moors murders' case.[2] In 1969 Myra Hindley asked Frank to help her to gain permission to see Brady. Frank, at first hesitant, agreed to see Myra and has championed her cause ever since. Elizabeth had no such hesitation; she was strongly opposed to Frank's having anything to do with either prisoner. 'I wanted him to keep his hands clean of these monsters'.[3] Myra Hindley eventually convinced Frank that she was a reformed character and he, following his deeply held Christian conviction that no human being is beyond forgiveness, undertook to campaign for her parole. His support for Hindley is also based on justice; she is among the handful of UK prisoners serving a life sentence who have been given no date for the consideration of parole.

Despite her original opposition, Elizabeth was persuaded by Frank to visit Hindley in 1976; since then Elizabeth has made further visits, entered a correspondence and come to like and accept Myra Hindley in her new guise of sincere Catholic and model prisoner. However, Myra Hindley's release is not the burning issue for Elizabeth that it remains for Frank.

In 1971, a time when both Elizabeth and Frank felt raw from the mauling given to Frank by the press, Frank received an outstanding tribute. He was made a Knight of the Garter, the highest honour in the gift of the Queen. The Order, founded by Edward III in 1348, is limited to twenty-four non-royal members in addition to certain members of the royal family. Frank was thrilled; accompanied proudly by Elizabeth, he was installed at the Garter ceremony in June 1971 at St George's Chapel, Windsor.

Elizabeth's pride is well founded. Frank's achievements speak for themselves: a double first, a distinguished don, the chairman of an important company, a Cabinet minister who had been appointed to office by one of this century's most outstanding prime ministers, a writer of repute. His courage as a champion of the underdog and defender of lost causes has become a byword. Yet Frank's gifts are counterbalanced by an impracticality that is the frequent butt of his own and his family's jokes. He cannot make a cup of tea, sharpen a pencil or carry a tray without risking dropping it. More fundamentally, his achievements have failed to restore the self-confidence that was so early undermined by a mother who rarely praised and often ignored him. It is generally agreed that he could never have fulfilled his potential without the love, confidence and happiness that Elizabeth has inspired throughout their long and mutually fulfilling marriage.

Elizabeth and Frank have built their life together on firm shared principles. They have always believed in the sanctity of marriage, which for them is a lifelong commitment. They have enjoyed a happy, normal sex life together. Sadly for Elizabeth, not all her children's marriages have achieved such stability and happiness. Untouched by the changes in morality herself, she had no idea that the permissive society of the 1960s had had any serious effect on her children. Thus Antonia's decision to leave Hugh Fraser for the playwright Harold Pinter in 1975 was a bombshell for Elizabeth, for whom Antonia had always been 'our wonder child'. The break-up of Antonia's marriage was blazoned all over the tabloids, together with any connected or disconnected scandal that could be pinned on her. So scurrilous was the gossip that for Christmas Antonia gave her mother the three brass monkeys, 'see no evil', 'hear no evil' and 'speak no evil'.

Determined to keep all the family relationships in balance, Elizabeth played the role of peacemaker in the family and welcomed and accepted Harold Pinter into the family circle while maintaining her affection for Hugh Fraser. When he became ill with cancer Hugh was visited in hospital by all his children, who were devoted to him, and by Antonia. Hugh died in 1984 aged sixty-six; Elizabeth, Frank, Antonia and all the children were at his funeral and at his memorial service.

Some years earlier, Kevin, whom Elizabeth regarded with special affection as 'her Benjamin', had grieved his mother by openly living with his fiancée, Ruth Jackson. Elizabeth explained to Kevin and Ruth that although she accepted their decision, she could not condone sex outside marriage; according to her deeply held beliefs they were disobeying the law of God. Kevin and Ruth were married in Oxford in 1972 where Kevin was completing his studies. Twelve years later, the marriage in severe difficulties, Elizabeth had a meeting with Ruth, to whom she is devoted, in an attempt to help restore the marriage. When she realised that this was not possible she concentrated on preventing the family relationships from souring. When Kevin told his mother that he was going to find it very difficult to be a good Catholic, she replied, 'Maybe you can't be a good Catholic. Maybe you can only be a bad Catholic.'[4]

By 1984, when Kevin and Ruth divorced, Elizabeth had had to become resigned to the broken marriages of her children. A year or two before Kevin's divorce, Judith left Alec Kazantzis; she now lives with Irving Weinman. In 1980 Paddy and Mary divorced; on medical advice Paddy also retired from the Bar.

Elizabeth has been a great support to Paddy and his three sons. She used a considerable part of her literary earnings to provide private education for Paddy's children, and in 1980, after he had lost his marital home, she provided a flat for him. All these failed marriages caused Elizabeth much sorrow, but she has the objectivity to recognise that those of her children who parted from their original spouses have become happier people; in each case the second attempt has proved to be a lasting relationship.

Although the leisure time Elizabeth anticipated did not materialise, she has achieved a simpler domestic life. In 1978 adaptations were undertaken at Bernhurst to provide two self-contained units: 'Frontstairs' for herself and Frank, and 'Backstairs' for the children and their families. 'Granny, you are lucky to have two kitchens,' commented Kevin's seven-year-old Hermione after her first visit to 'Backstairs'. 'Lucky!', retorted Elizabeth. 'If I had two playrooms, that would be lucky!' At Bernhurst she continues to avoid cooking, which, along with most of the domestic chores, is done by Gwen Brown and Ellen Grinter valiantly who took over from Popey.

Gardening has become an increasingly absorbing occupation for Elizabeth, who has been wholly responsible for the present form of Bernhurst garden. When she arrived in 1950 the garden had been largely steam-rollered by its wartime occupants. There were no hedges nor paths nor flower-beds; the few azaleas and rhododendrons were straggly and unkempt and the lawns non-existent. By then she had some experience of gardening, but the five-acre Bernhurst garden was on a far bigger scale than anything that Elizabeth had been responsible for before. Nor was it easy to find advice in those days. Elizabeth relied principally on a nurseryman at Tunbridge Wells, but he was not much more knowledgable than she was. One flowering shrub bought to grow to about three feet soon reached the height of a sapling; but for Elizabeth not knowing how the plants would turn out has always been part of the attraction of gardening. She introduced brick and closely mown grass paths, which she copied from her mother's garden in Kent. Noting the effectiveness of white flowers in the neighbouring garden of Sissinghurst Castle, she made a feature of white. The whole is designed around a three-hundred-year-old great oak, a wellingtonia and a monkey puzzle tree, the three trees that dominate the garden. At first she was able to employ a full-time gardener, but since 1995 she has relied on one day's work a week from the incomparable Derek Westgate. She is never happier than when she herself is at work, but since her balance was affected by a back operation in 1988, she has had regretfully to abandon digging.

Bernhurst garden is highly popular with the grandchildren, who are frequent visitors. They have had to learn to respect her work time. She keeps up a large correspondence, writing frequently to grandchildren away at boarding-school. She can be quite sharp. Richard, the eldest son of Paddy and Mary, wrote her an illegible letter. Elizabeth wrote to thank him, but suggested that next time it would be much more interesting for her if he sent a letter she could read.

Most of the grandchildren have confided in Elizabeth at one time or another. Serious boy- and girlfriends are introduced and her advice is often taken. One of Paddy's children explained how he had found a marvellous girl but he was not going to propose until he had managed to save more money. 'Be careful,' cautioned Elizabeth, 'or she may be snapped up by somebody else.' She underlined her warning by relating how she had had to wait for Frank because he was fearful of becoming trapped. The pair were married before the year was out.

Like all grandmothers Elizabeth enjoys telling the old family stories and always has a photograph album to hand. The best-loved tale is that of her own father, who fell fully dressed from a punt into the river Medway when she was a child. Family theatricals are also part of the Bernhurst tradition; they are specially popular because Elizabeth allows the children the freedom of her wardrobe and her dressing-table. This supplements the dressing-up trunk in which clothes have accumulated over the years; the oldest garment in it is a diminutive black bodice that belonged to Great-Aunt Caroline.

Elizabeth is at pains not to interfere and usually advocates a policy of inaction, in the firm belief that, if left alone, most difficulties sort themselves out. She made an exception in the case of Nat Billington, Rachel's eldest son, who was failing at school, although he was clearly very intelligent. Elizabeth gave him a computer for his eleventh birthday and after that he never looked back. When he was twenty-two he set up his own computer company with a couple of friends.

There is a sweet shop at the end of Bernhurst drive; trips to the shop to buy something from its excellent 'pick-and-mix' selection are a favourite occupation both for Elizabeth and the grandchildren, so much so that their parents have stepped in and imposed a 25p limit on each child. Elizabeth has bowed to their wishes, but she makes sure that the house is well stocked with all the children's favourites.

Weekends spent 'Backstairs' at Bernhurst are hugely popular, specially with the youngest children of Kevin and his beloved wife Clare, Ben, Hermione and Dominic, who as the car draws up, always race to the front of the house to find their grandparents. Once in 1995 they rushed back again straight away, imploring Kevin and Clare to come with them but to 'be quiet'. The children led their parents to Frank's study, where on a sofa in front of the television they found Frank and Elizabeth sleeping peacefully – she with her head on his shoulder, he with his arm around her. These three children, the youngest of the twenty-six grandchildren, are keenly aware of their grandparents' mutual devotion and take delight in it. They danced on their toes with joy when describing how once they had found Elizabeth in the garden trimming Frank's hair.

Elizabeth is generally believed to have mellowed with age;

she gives no impression of impatience and now it is difficult to imagine her losing her temper. Age has also tempered her ambition and with more physical space and time she is now seldom frustrated. She has abandoned the attempt to publish *Letters from my Grandchildren*, a project she began after completing *Royal Throne*, mostly because it was clear that, as they were all from the same social background, their opinions were not sufficiently diverse to create an interesting book. Nevertheless, she continues to aim at a five- or six-hour working day and is never without some review or article to write. She continues to read the manuscripts produced by different members of her family, advises aspiring writers and is generous in writing introductions and recommendations. Naturally this work, although time-consuming and important to her, does not create the same pressure as that of her full-length books; in recent years therefore she has had more time for her family and friends. Her children were inclined to complain that they did not see enough of her; her grandchildren think she is perfect.

Elizabeth's third son, Michael, was the last to marry. Elizabeth and Frank did not meet his talented fiancée until they flew to Washington on the eve of his wedding day on 26th April 1980. Michael met Mimi Doak when he was First Secretary in the Washington Embassy, where he was again serving under Nicko Henderson, the Ambassador. Elizabeth and Frank arrived for a three-day stay on 24th April, but, knowing his mother, Michael had laid on a sightseeing tour for her. Elizabeth visited the Jefferson Monument, the recently opened wing of the National Gallery and George Washington's home at Mount Vernon. However, even Elizabeth, with her strong constitution, was tired out when she returned; she caught a cold on the plane and admitted to feeling wretched (*Diary*).

During the 1970s, when Elizabeth was writing her books on Wellington, Blunt and Byron, she was able to combine her love of travel with her research. In the 1980s, apart from the brief trip to Washington and one trip to South Africa to promote *Elizabeth R*, she travelled for pleasure only. For fifteen years (1979–94) she had a summer break as the guest of Antonia and Harold at the villa that they generally took on some island in the Mediterranean. Elizabeth was in her element on these Mediterranean holidays, which for her were marred only by Frank's absence. Rachel and Kevin Billington were frequently fellow guests. Elizabeth, stimulated by the literary discussions and play readings organised by Harold, always enjoyed herself. 'The company of those I love, and the sight of beautiful things and the feel of warm sun and water make me feel radiantly happy,' she confided to her diary. In 1986 the holiday nearly ended in tragedy when Kevin and Rachel were involved in a head-on collision on their way home. They owed their lives to the sheer weight of Kevin's old Mercedes in which they were travelling. Nevertheless, Kevin had to spend two weeks in hospital; Rachel escaped with severe bruising.

In 1994 Elizabeth regretfully explained to Antonia that she would not join her for a holiday again, as she could not continue to abandon Frank for a week each summer. Surprisingly, it was Harold who was the more disappointed. He regards his mother-in-law as 'a person of immense generosity and a true and constant equilibrium'.[5]

In October 1983 Elizabeth and Thomas spent a week in South Africa on a promotional tour for Elizabeth's biography of the Queen and Thomas' book on the Boer War. This was strenuous. Elizabeth nevertheless enjoyed it. She was particularly keen to see South Africa, the setting for *Jameson's Raid*, her first serious book, but she agreed to go only because Thomas was prepared to go with her. She described him as 'the most perfect and wonderful fellow-traveller, so euphoric and bursting with fascinating information' (*Diary*). She was then seventy-seven years old and frustrated by her deafness, a disability that has become an increasing handicap in her old age.

During the week Elizabeth gave a number of interviews and talks in Johannesburg, Durban and Cape Town; wherever she spoke she was asked how well she knew the Queen. 'Quite well,' she replied, and refused to expand. A referendum on constitutional change was imminent and was the main topic at any social gathering; greatly interested, she took part in the discussions, which added to her enjoyment of the visit. Elizabeth had been in contact with Frank throughout the trip, but was nevertheless thankful to get back to Chesil Court, where she found a 'welcome home' note pinned to the door.

Shortly after her return Elizabeth bowed to pressure from her family and her publishers, and began to write her own memoirs. She was reluctant to undertake the task because she believed that nothing of importance had happened in her life; furthermore, she is fundamentally uninterested in herself. Diana Cooper said of her, 'No one so successful was ever so unselfimportant', a remark that has often been quoted by Frank and more recently by Roy Jenkins during Elizabeth's ninetieth birthday party at the House of Lords on 12th September 1996.

Elizabeth has always been popular as a speaker and in consequence has been much in demand for lectures, especially on the subjects of her books. In 1977 she spoke entertainingly at Scotland Yard on 'The Duke of Wellington as co-founder with Robert Peel of the Metropolitan Police'. Occasionally Elizabeth has been asked to speak abroad. In October 1979 she was invited by the British Council to lecture to the Waterloo Committee on 'The problems of the Battle'. She enjoyed this, finding it a comparatively easy subject for her Belgian audience to understand; she described several disconnected episodes, without the need to sustain an argument. In September 1992 she was invited to give a lecture in Trim, county Meath, as a part of the town's Wellington Festival celebrations. As a small boy Wellington had spent a brief period at the Diocesan School in Trim, for which he was later a Member of Parliament. The lecture was a great success, largely because she departed from her prepared text in order to comment on the achievements of the burghers of Trim, which had been mentioned at length by several preceding speakers.

In 1982 at the London School of Economics she gave a talk on Beatrice Webb, causing much amusement with her description of her first meeting, when they had nearly come to blows over a disputed hotel bedroom. She was aware of the need to develop her speaking technique and, impressed by that of Noel Annan, the president of the London Library, deliberately assumed a more dramatic style. In 1988, on Waterloo Day, 18th June, she gave the inaugural lecture to mark the reopening of the refurbished Apsley House, once known as 'No. 1 London', bought by the first Duke of Wellington as his town house in 1817.[6] Dressed in the Life Guards jacket that had belonged to her father-in-law and wearing long black boots, Elizabeth strode on to the platform, where she ranted and raved and even acted out some of the dialogues. Her success with this technique was such that she used it on many subsequent occasions.

In 1981 Elizabeth and Frank celebrated their golden wedding. All the family were present, including Mimi and Michael, who came from America bringing with them six-week-old Alexandra, their first child. Elizabeth arranged for Patrick Lichfield to photograph her family; he had to use a naval whistle to establish order among his thirty-nine sitters. The anniversary, marked by parties, presents – many of them plants and shrubs for the garden – and speeches left Elizabeth feeling grateful and proud. During the next two decades, anniversaries, birthdays, weddings and christenings were to follow in almost nonstop succession. The publication of *The Pebbled Shore*, Elizabeth's memoirs, had been planned to coincide with her eightieth birthday, making for a double celebration. For this Frank gave her a bright red satin jumpsuit. The following May Elizabeth was thrilled by the arrival of Stella, her first great-grandchild, the daughter of Antonia's second daughter, Flora.

On Thursday 15th October 1987 Elizabeth was awoken by wind rattling the windows of her London flat; she went back to sleep, unaware that a hurricane was devastating the South-east of England. She woke to find her planned weekend at Bernhurst was out of the question; railway lines and roads were blocked with fallen trees and the electricity supply had failed.[7] She managed to get to Bernhurst the following week and was appalled by the havoc she found. About sixty trees were lost, including Scots pines, birches that had been transplanted from her mother's garden in Kent, a scarlet oak, a Japanese maple, apple trees and a walnut tree half uprooted that had just started to bear. Nevertheless, Elizabeth could consider herself fortunate. The three major trees, although severely battered and diminished by the loss of huge branches, were all still standing. During the next several weeks various members of the family formed working parties to clear the debris. Many trees were replaced and, seven years on, after considerable expense and hard work, Elizabeth was able to appreciate that the storm had brought some improvement. 'Before the storm one admired the garden and the view separately. Now, with so many of the obscuring Scots pines down, the two are viewed together, each made more entrancing by the other' (Diary).

While the garden had survived a severe ordeal, Elizabeth had hers yet to come. Just before Christmas 1988, without warning, she was struck down with acute back pain and was found to be suffering from a meningioma, a benign tumour, on her spine, which had been stealthily growing to the size of a ripe tomato. This was successfully removed by Mr David Uttley, her neurosurgeon. He was not sanguine, declaring that her chances of a full recovery were 'bleak indeed'. Elizabeth was to confound him, for she brought 'courage, verve, a sense of discipline and determination, which contributed significantly to her recovery'.[8]

Elizabeth spent six weeks in hospital, then, encouraged by

her brother John, himself a physician, discharged herself. John had remained a great support to her, although busy lives had prevented them from seeing a great deal of each other. Three months after she left hospital, during a final check-up, she complained of having to walk with the aid of two sticks. She was told that she should consider herself fortunate to be on her feet and not in a wheelchair; she must acclimatise herself to walking with sticks for she would have to rely on them for the rest of her life. 'Are you depressed about using sticks?' Antonia asked. 'I would be if I believed a word of it,' said Elizabeth. Less than four months later Elizabeth was presiding at the launch of her *Oxford Book of Royal Anecdotes*. She was then still in some pain and was using a stick, but her wit was not dulled. 'A kind of poor man's Madame Tussauds without the waxworks' was her description of the building near the Barbican (since closed down), where Oxford University Press had arranged the launch; a location that she found both inconvenient and ugly, though the party was spirited.

The following summer she went away with the Pinters as usual, resumed her swimming, which certainly aided her recovery, and by the end of the year had discarded her sticks. She did make two small concessions to her back: she bought a new mattress for the flat and she traded in her old car for a Colt Mitsubishi, which had power steering. She was to drive for four more years until the age of eighty-eight when, to her great regret, her licence was withdrawn owing to glaucoma.

In 1993 Elizabeth received a further honour, which to her delight included Frank. Lucy Willis, the winner of the British Petroleum Portrait Painters Award, received an unusual commission to paint a double portrait of Elizabeth and Frank. (The Award, open to painters under forty, offers a prize of £10,000 plus a commission for a contemporary portrait chosen by the National Portrait Gallery.) Double portraits are notoriously difficult to paint, and Lucy's task was made no easier because Frank, anxious to return to the House of Lords, fidgeted throughout the sittings. Worse, he managed to step into the palette, which had been left in the flat overnight, splashing paint all over the carpet and his trousers. No second pair was available. When he left on time to be in the House of Lords by noon the next day, his trousers were still damp and smelt distinctly of turpentine.

The portrait is generally thought to be excellent of Frank, less good of Elizabeth, her self-effacement inevitably making her likeness more difficult to capture. What the artist has achieved is the air of contented partnership, emphasised by careful composition. Elizabeth and Frank sit side by side on matching chairs, in reflective pose, their hands tranquilly folded.

11

Author of Distinction

I Major Historical Biographies

In the light of Elizabeth's success with the first volume of the
Wellington biography and of *Victoria RI*, it is easy to forget that
she never studied modern history. Her degree in Literae
Humaniores, however, included the study of ancient history,
which, she claims, gave an excellent grounding. Frank also
helped: for several years he had taught modern history at Christ
Church and was the author of the scholarly *Peace by Ordeal*.
Her greatest asset however, was the ability to cut loose from
the family around her to give undivided attention to the work
in hand. This, a skill she had practised throughout her life, was
to become increasingly important after 1953 when, at the age
of forty-seven, she began to write seriously.

At one time Frank believed his wife needed a room of her
own, out of bounds to the children, in which she could work;
but Elizabeth did not want to be shut away, preferring interruption to isolation. Now and then she might make herself
deaf to the demands of the children, but she never withdrew
and did not have a room, nor even a desk or table dedicated
solely to her work.

Much as she enjoys the process of writing, Elizabeth is equally
attracted by research. In 1956, fired by her recent Greek cruise,
she was looking forward to working on the Chamberlain papers

in preparation for a biography of her great-uncle, Joseph Chamberlain. Her mother had known him well and as a small child Elizabeth had met him, although by then he had suffered a stroke and was in failing health; given this personal background, Elizabeth believed that he would make an ideal subject for her first biography. A family connection, Terence Maxwell, son-in-law of Austen Chamberlain, was in charge of the Chamberlain archive. Before approaching Terence for access to the papers, Elizabeth spent five months familiarising herself with Joseph Chamberlain's background.

When she finally made her request to see the archive, it was declined. The archive was to be a gift to Birmingham University, which was then in the process of building a new library; in the interim the papers had been lodged for safety in a bank.[1] Having studied long and hard, Elizabeth was not prepared to abandon the project, but without access to Joseph Chamberlain's papers, her book would lack the necessary authenticity and ran the risk of bearing too close a resemblance to J. L. Garvin's official biography, *Life of Joseph Chamberlain* (published by Macmillan in 1932). Her solution was to narrow the canvas in order to concentrate on a single and highly controversial episode, the Jameson raid of 1897. If this free-booting attempt to seize Johannesburg had been successful, Transvaal and the Orange Free State would probably have been absorbed into the British Empire before the end of the nine-teenth century.

As Secretary of State for the Colonies in the Conservative government of Lord Salisbury, Joseph Chamberlain denounced the raid and set up a committee of inquiry. The point at issue was the question of Chamberlain's own complicity. The committee of inquiry totally exonerated Chamberlain and, for his biographer, Garvin, that had been the end of the matter. However, South African critics, most notably the writer Jean van der Poel, viewed with great suspicion Chamberlain's membership of the committee that had exonerated him, judging that Chamberlain was in it 'up to the neck' and that the inquiry was simply a whitewash. In her attempt to get at the truth Elizabeth became absorbed in the politics of South Africa.

Her findings were published in 1960. *Jameson's Raid* was well received and a revised edition was reissued in 1982. Elizabeth was considered to have told a complicated episode skilfully. E. E. Y. Hales, writing in *The Tablet* on 17th July 1982, noted 'her eye for illustrative detail, her gift for rapid narrative, her capacity to assemble, digest and assess information from a wide range of sources . . .' She, on the other hand, was dissatisfied with her work because she had departed from the chronological order of events, an error she never repeated. Elizabeth worked her apprenticeship on *Jameson's Raid*, learning to handle historical documents and to use chronology as a scaffold for her narrative. By becoming familiar with the Victorian age she also laid the foundations for her first major work, the biography of Queen Victoria.

This subject was suggested to Elizabeth by her agent, Graham Watson. She had been intrigued by Queen Victoria since her school days at Headington, when she had been given Lytton Strachey's *Queen Victoria* (Chatto and Windus, 1921) as a history prize and been carried away by the book. Strachey presented the Queen as an amusing, lively human being, in contrast to the general perception of a dull, forbidding ruler who was never amused. There had been no recent serious study of Victoria and if access could be gained to the unpublished material in the royal archives at Windsor, the book would offer a challenge to her as an author and a plum for her publisher. Access to the royal archives, which include the private papers of members of the royal family, is restricted to established writers researching a specific subject. Browsing through the archive in search of a likely incident or personality is not permitted. The first step for any would-be researcher is the submission of published work to the Queen's advisers. Fortunately for Elizabeth, Martin Charteris was a friend of long standing. She submitted *Jameson's Raid* to the private secretary, Michael Adeane, which established her credentials. She was successfully over her first hurdle.

In conversation later with Norman St John Stevas, Elizabeth was surprised and pleased to discover that he was also fascinated by Queen Victoria. He owned a pair of black silk, white-soled stockings that had been worn by the Queen.[2] This was a rather more interesting relic than Elizabeth's original photograph of Queen Victoria in a donkey-cart. 'Are you writing a life of Queen Victoria?' she asked. He was. 'Are you in the royal archives?' He was not. Norman St John Stevas abandoned his attempt to write the biography.

For the next two years Elizabeth's working days were divided between Windsor Castle and the Chelsea flat. Parking her Mini under the southern bastion of the Castle, she collected a large brass key from the livery porter, climbed three hundred steps to the Round Tower and let herself into the small room reserved for her. This room, smelling faintly but unmistakably of gas, overlooked the great courtyard, where bands paraded and feet stamped. Elizabeth was witnessing scenes and hearing sounds that would have been familiar to Queen Victoria. The one problem with the room was the chair, which induced instant backache. This was easily remedied. During her first lunch break she went to Woolworths and bought a folding beach chair, low enough to enable her to work with her papers spread across the floor.

Among Elizabeth's principal sources were the diaries of Queen Victoria. These she found disappointing, owing to thorough expurgation by the Queen's youngest daughter, Princess Beatrice, who had been entrusted with the task of copying the original text. Princess Beatrice omitted all comments and events that she considered unseemly and the result was eighty exercise books filled with Beatrice's even, legible and flawless handwriting. The content of the original diaries will never be known, since these were destroyed; only the diaries kept by the young Victoria before her marriage at the age of twenty escaped censorship. Beatrice's recopying was not wholly disastrous. Queen Victoria's handwriting, already almost illegible, was not improved by the use of pale blue ink on thin blue writing paper. She also 'economised' by writing on both sides of the paper. Despite years of deciphering Frank's almost illegible writing, Elizabeth was often defeated and had to call on the librarian, Robert Mackworth-Young. In addition to the diaries, her main sources were contemporary letters and journals. Queen Victoria's letters to the Princess Royal, the Kronberg letters, the Greville memoirs and the Ponsonby papers were among the most informative.[3]

The amount of potential source material was formidable; Elizabeth persevered without research assistance. For the first year she painstakingly copied everything out in longhand, until she realised that her neighbour in the next room was dictating into a tape recorder. Having obtained permission, she arrived for the following session armed with a similar machine. Delighted by the speed with which the tape recorder enabled her to progress, she ignored a curious smell and continued dictating her notes until the machine began to give off clouds of smoke. Elizabeth had failed to discover that the Tower still worked on direct current (DC), rather than the modern alternating current (AC) for which contemporary machines are designed. Elizabeth continued to use a tape recorder, later transcribing her taped notes into a variety of different-coloured notebooks according to chronological order. She writes her first draft in exercise books, leaving alternate pages blank to allow for editing; this edited text is dictated on to a tape and finally given to a secretary to be typed.

Reflecting on her writing methods (*The Pebbled Shore*, pp. 330–31), Elizabeth has observed that she likes to see the subjects in her mind's eye, as well as to see the actual letters they wrote, the clothes they wore, the parks they walked in. She was stimulated by working at Windsor. It was easy to make herself familiar with Victoria's pattern of life. 'In order to enter into another human life I have to follow as far as possible in the person's footsteps. I look at the houses, gardens, scenery they knew.' For Victoria's biography this involved journeys through England and Scotland, notably to Osborne, on the Isle of Wight, Balmoral, and to the royal mausoleum at Frogmore where Prince Albert and later the Queen were buried.

Elizabeth's empathy with Victoria increased. On 14th December 1962 she read Victoria's diary for 14th December 1861, the day on which her beloved Albert finally succumbed to the illness that was to kill him (probably typhoid). Such was Elizabeth's identification with her subject that she found herself increasingly concerned for Frank's welfare, fussing about such small matters as changing out of wet socks that would surely give him a chill!

In 1964, after four years of unremitting work, the book was completed, leaving Elizabeth with the final hurdle of royal approval. What would be made of a portrait of Queen Victoria whose husband subjected intimate relations with her to logical analysis and presented them to her under numbered headings?[4] And what of a royal quarrel over the health of the Princess Royal, Vicky, which culminated in a bitter note from Albert: '... take the child away and do as you like and if she dies you will have it on your conscience'?[5] In the event Elizabeth was merely asked to excise two minor references; in every other respect, her six-hundred-page biography of Queen Victoria was acceptable to that monarch's great-great-granddaughter, the present Queen Elizabeth II.

Victoria RI was published by Weidenfeld & Nicolson in 1964, to a rapturous reception. For the historian A. J. P. Taylor the book was 'suffused with sympathy and understanding' (*Observer Review*, 13th September 1964). James Pope-Hennessey noted approvingly that '... Lady Longford makes no bones about her own warm feelings for the complex and contradictory character of the Queen' (*Sunday Times*, same date). She had successfully kept her subject in the limelight, enabling such giants as Wellington, Palmerston, Gladstone and Disraeli to make constant appearances without upstaging the Queen. *Victoria RI* was awarded the James Tait Black Memorial prize for non-fiction and enjoyed just as much success in America.

Elizabeth now began to cast around for a further subject for biography. She considered Mary, Queen of Scots, but doubted the wisdom of abandoning the Victorian era, which she was beginning to make her own, for one of which she had no knowledge. George Weidenfeld suggested the Duke of Wellington, who had been something of a father figure to the young Queen Victoria. This was an attractive prospect, but Elizabeth doubted whether Gerald Wellesley, the seventh Duke and custodian of the Wellington papers, would entrust them to her. She also feared that, as the marriage between the Duke of Wellington and Frank's great-great-aunt, Kitty Pakenham, had been such a mistake, the Wellesleys would suspect bias from any Pakenham.

As it happened, the Duke had invited Sir Philip Magnus to undertake a biography based on the family archive, but the invitation had been refused, and the Duke was delighted that Elizabeth was prepared to step into the breach. He hoped the biography could be published in 1969, the bicentenary of the birth of the Great Duke. This deadline and Elizabeth's commitment to it were the determining factors in her decision not to stand for the post of principal of St Hilda's.

From 1964 Elizabeth was absorbed in the Wellington archive. The Wellington papers were divided between Apsley House and Stratfield Saye, Hampshire, the country seat of the Dukes of Wellington, which had been given to the first Duke in recognition of the victory at Waterloo. Luckily this time she was allowed to take material away. Her aim was to use every available document, military, political or personal, that cast light upon the character of the Duke. The Queen's Press Secretary, Charles Anson, has vivid memories of staying at

Bernhurst during this period and of meeting Elizabeth in the garden with a trug on each arm, one filled with flowers, the other with Wellington papers.[6] She was never parted from the documents: whether in Chelsea or Sussex, the papers went with her.

But the archive was not enough. If Elizabeth was to understand the complexities of Wellington's military campaigns she must see the battlefields for herself. This was of particular importance in the case of the Peninsular Campaign, which Elizabeth saw as the turning-point in the ultimate defeat of Napoleon. Before visiting any of the battlefields she studied manuals on military tactics. Only then did she visit all the European battlefields on which the Duke had been engaged. At each site, she drew sketch maps, took photographs and made copious notes.

One of these was Torres Vedras, a town of the most elaborate and secret defences, comprising over 150 fortified sites. 'Torres Vedras – the old towers – was one of the most ancient towns of Portugal. It had its river, the Zizandre, its aqueduct, its Moorish castle high on a hill and on another hill opposite, at the top of a serpentine road, the fourteenth-century Chapel of St Vincent' (*Wellington: The Years of the Sword*, p. 278). In the autumn of 1810 the lines of Torres Vedras had held the French back for a few vital weeks, allowing the British and their allies to turn the tide of the Peninsular War and begin their advance to victory.

The complexities of the Peninsular War and the lines of Torres Vedras were such that one visit was not sufficient. Elizabeth managed to secure funding from the Gulbenkian Foundation for a further visit to the Iberian peninsula in 1966, on which she was accompanied by Catherine, her youngest daughter. At this point, with the writing well advanced, it was becoming apparent that a satisfactory biography of the Duke of Wellington could not be encompassed within a single volume. Moreover, much research remained to be done, and it was clear that only the Duke's life up to the time of Waterloo could be completed within the deadline. A further volume would be required.

Wellington: The Years of the Sword was published in October 1969, ready for the centenary year and in the meantime for Christmas sales. Three weeks before the launch of the book Elizabeth was involved in a car accident, which could have proved fatal. Driving her Mini to Bernhurst, she pulled out to overtake, realised it was unsafe and, pulling back, collided with the car behind. Her own car was a write-off. Elizabeth suffered internal bleeding as well as damage to her spine, and was told to spend several weeks on her back in hospital. She was courteous but adamant in her insistence on returning home. There she was to remain for the next four weeks, while Rachel deputised at a number of events planned for the launch of the book.

The reviews were universally favourable. The Cambridge historian Professor J. H. Plumb admired the book's 'immense readability and its sympathetic understanding of one of England's great folk heroes' (*New York Times*, 1st March 1970). Elizabeth was justly praised for the depth of her research – she had tapped no fewer than two hundred and fifty sources of original material. Notable among them was the private journal of Kitty Pakenham, the Duke's unhappy wife.

The book was awarded a prize of £200 by the *Yorkshire Post* as 'Best Book of the Year'. Elizabeth spent the money on buying an original note written by the Duke at 3 a.m. on 18th June 1815, before the Battle of Waterloo had begun. The note is addressed to the British ambassador in Brussels, Sir Charles Stuart, asking him to try to keep the British civilians quiet and calm. She had previously been offered first refusal of this historic letter, but had turned it down because of its expense. Elizabeth was elected a member of the Royal Society of Literature and awarded an honorary Doctorate in Literature by the University of Sussex.

Success was gratifying, but the second volume had still to be written. From 1815 until his death in 1852 the Duke remained a prominent figure in public life. He served twice as Prime Minister and once as Foreign Secretary. Still, there was a possibility that, however skilful Elizabeth's treatment, this part of the Duke's life could seem an anticlimax after Waterloo.

Most of the research for the second volume had already been done. Elizabeth enthusiastically undertook what remained, finding it marvellously restful to be reading again, to be 'imbibing instead of throwing out'.[7] She bypassed the temptation to weigh the soldier against the politician, concentrating on producing a portrait of a patriot driven by a sense of duty, and revealing a man of wit, common sense and feeling. She retold many of the well-loved Wellington stories, including the advice given to Queen Victoria in 1851. No one had found a way of getting rid of the sparrows infesting the Crystal Palace built by Paxton in Hyde Park to house the Great Exhibition. 'Try sparrow-hawks, Ma'am,' said Wellington, and the problem was solved. In 1972 *Wellington: Pillar of State* was published, consolidating Elizabeth's reputation. At one point the book was selling over a thousand copies a week and many critics considered it to be even more compelling than *Wellington: The Years of the Sword*.

The subjects of her later books have varied widely, for Elizabeth has often responded to requests and commissions. Many of her works have been concerned with members of the royal family; she has also produced anthologies and written her own memoirs. In this discussion, her writings are grouped according to subject rather than in chronological order.

Elizabeth wrote one more significant biography, that of the eccentric and minor poet Wilfrid Scawen Blunt (1840–1922), although some found it difficult to see his attraction for her. Blunt was an insatiable womaniser, dubbed by some as 'the poor man's Byron', an Arabist and an anti-imperialist, who, with the help of his wife, Lady Anne Noel, Byron's granddaughter, founded a distinguished Arab stud farm.

Blunt's life in no way measured up to that of Queen Victoria or the first Duke of Wellington, but the process of researching it held appeal for Elizabeth. She would again be working on original papers that had previously been unavailable, and she would have to travel extensively in pursuit of her subject.

Blunt's private papers, which included details of his numerous affairs, were in Cambridge in the Fitzwilliam Museum. A fifty-year embargo had been imposed at his death in 1922 since when little had been written about him and public interest in him had waned. On the expiry of the embargo, the syndics of the Fitzwilliam (the University's committee of management) wanted to make the Blunt archive generally available, but first to commission an authorised biography. The director, Professor Michael Jaffé, knew Elizabeth and sought her opinion of the eccentric poet. She had encountered Blunt while researching *Victoria RI* and had been favourably impressed by his outspoken and critical view of the Queen's imperialist stance. Jaffé was satisfied by this response and Elizabeth was commissioned to write the authorised biography.

Blunt's colourful character was intriguing, but Elizabeth's long-standing love of Byron also drew her towards Anne Noel, Blunt's wife and Byron's granddaughter. The lure of untouched primary sources was irresistible. Since Blunt had been an explorer, and had bought property in Cairo, Elizabeth would probably have to pursue her research in India, North Africa and the Middle East. But as her research proceeded the appeal of Blunt waned; this was '[the only time I have felt] ... my empathy oozing away while in the midst of writing a biography ... Fortunately my sympathies returned as [Blunt's] physical powers failed' (*The Pebbled Shore*, p. 332).

In February 1977 Elizabeth visited India, taking with her Rachel Billington, her third daughter. Michael, who was then serving in the British High Commission in Delhi, made the arrangements and even organised an expedition to Calcutta, where Elizabeth and Rachel were able to visit the Mother House of the Missionaries of Charity and meet their founder, Mother

Teresa.[8] Elizabeth's long-standing friendship with Malcolm Muggeridge and his wife ensured a warm welcome from Mother Teresa. 'We congratulated her on her work. "We must not spoil it . . . ," replied Mother Teresa. "How could you?" "By saying that we are doing it ourselves"' (*Diary*, 23rd February 1977). In this way, Mother Teresa, by insisting that God did all the work, humbly deflected praise from herself. Before leaving they wanted to make a donation but finding no alms box referred to Mother Teresa, who very simply held out her cupped hands, which they filled. As was her custom, Elizabeth kept a detailed diary of the visit to India, noting how greatly the country had changed since Blunt's visit in 1883.

Part of the appeal of a biography for Elizabeth is the detective work. The object of her visit to Egypt in January 1978 was to find 'Sheyk Obeyd', the area on the outskirts of Cairo where Blunt had bought a garden and built a house. After separating from her husband in 1906, Lady Anne Blunt had lived there until her death in 1917. Against the odds, Elizabeth found both the garden and Anne Blunt's grave.

Elizabeth's party, which included Rachel and Thomas, also visited the Pyramids, although Elizabeth declined the opportunity to climb them. While the others did, she mounted a camel but found that the stirrups were too long, the pommel tiny and there were no reins. She did not enjoy the experience, admitting, 'I would never have done my camel act except that I felt I must experience something, if only a phantasm, of Lady Anne's 2000-mile journey across the Arabian desert of Nejd' (*Diary*, 27th January 1978).

The biography of Blunt presented two major problems. Elizabeth had difficulty in disentangling and explaining his endless and complex affairs with women many of whom were related to one another. Blunt had a penchant for saintly women such as Minnie Pollen, who bore him an illegitimate child when she was in her mid-thirties and had been married for nearly twenty years. Inevitably Elizabeth made some embarrassing discoveries about illegitimate children from the intimate diaries that Blunt had managed to keep secret. She proved that Lady Mary Lyon, the daughter of Lady Elcho, was in fact the child of Wilfrid Blunt; and that Clementine Churchill, wife of Sir Winston Churchill, who was the child of Lady Blanche, was in fact the natural daughter of Bay Middleton rather than of Sir Henry Hozier, Lady Blanche's husband. Lady Anne Blunt's papers caused practical difficulties; they were held in the British Library where staff shortages led to endless delays.

On 17th August 1977, 'Blunt's 137th birthday', as she noted in her diary, Elizabeth began to write. Some months later she handed nine chapters to Antonia, a dependable family critic, awaiting her daughter's verdict in some trepidation – she never felt confident about her success in dealing with Blunt. In July 1979 *A Pilgrimage of Passion* was published and for three weeks it was on the bestseller list. Some of Elizabeth's misgivings were, however, reflected in less favourable notices. Rebecca West expressed amazement at Elizabeth's liking for the profligate, and Robert Blake, writing in the *Illustrated London News*, complained that she had failed to explain Blunt's anti-imperialism. If this biography did not fully measure up to her previous works, the fault perhaps lay with the choice of subject, rather than with the author herself.

II Miscellanea

In 1974 Elizabeth brought Victoria's family up to date with *The Royal House of Windsor*. She was then approached by the Winston Churchill Foundation of the United States, founded in 1959 to provide scholarships and visiting fellowships for Americans at Churchill College, Cambridge, and was asked to provide the letterpress for a pictorial biography to mark the centenary of Sir Winston's birth, 30th November 1874. A brief linking text, enlivened by anecdotes, was required. Elizabeth was well suited to the task, having visited the Churchills at Chartwell, their country home, on several occasions and been present at Churchill's funeral service. She fulfilled the commission admirably, providing psychological insights and personal reminiscences with wit and skill.

Another of Elizabeth's heroes was the poet Lord Byron. Although he had died in 1824, before Victoria came to the throne, he was so much revered by the Victorians that she had learnt a lot about him while working on her first biography. She was therefore delighted to learn that the Byron Society, which had lapsed for a time, had been reconstituted. She joined the Society and not long after, at the request of Professor Plumb, began work on a biography of the poet as part of an American series of Great Lives.

Greece figured so large in Byron's life that Elizabeth felt the need to trace his footsteps there. Taking her recently widowed sister, Kitty, with her, she joined members of the Byron Society on their visit to Greece in 1973. At this time she was also asked to co-operate with Jorge Lewinski, a professional photographer, to produce *Byron's Greece*, a description of Byron's journeys of 1809–11 and 1823–4, commissioned to coincide with the 150th anniversary of the poet's death at Missolonghi in 1824. This was obviously an attractive assignment for Elizabeth. She and Jorge travelled to Greece with members of the Byron Society, and, determined to miss none of the social activities, she caught up on her notes for the book at night. *Byron's Greece* received a good press. The biography of Byron, published in 1976 for the American market (and also in the UK), was successful too.

In 1979 Elizabeth was co-opted by Bamber Gascoigne to write the text of *Images of Chelsea*, another pictorial book, part of the ambitious *Images of London* programme for which purpose Gascoigne had set up the St Helena Press. The idea was to reproduce and catalogue every known print of a particular area up to 1860. Elizabeth, who had been fascinated by Chelsea since she first went to live there, found this another most congenial task, which she accomplished with her usual competence and style.

Eminent Victorian Women, published in 1982, was another book for which the research gave Elizabeth great pleasure, partly because she was so familiar with the period. She was aware that for Victorian women it was social death to step outside the stereotypical ideal of wife and mother, as exemplified by Queen Victoria. She therefore chose eleven women who, despite the odds, managed to change society. These included famous names such as Florence Nightingale and George Eliot, along with less well-known ones such as Harriet Beecher Stowe, the American author (including of *Uncle Tom's Cabin*) whose writing helped to abolish slavery, and Annie Besant, who fought for birth control. The book provoked great interest, especially among women.

Elizabeth was now seventy-five years old and there was speculation that this would be her final work. But she had already embarked on a biography of Queen Elizabeth II, which she planned to publish in 1983, the thirtieth anniversary of the Queen's coronation. She has always insisted that writing a book fulfilled a genuine physical need (*Sunday Times*, 8th April 1990), and she satisfied this need by producing seven more books over the next twelve years.

The Pebbled Shore, her memoirs, was the only book that Elizabeth was genuinely reluctant to write, and she did so only at the insistence of her family, reinforced by Weidenfeld and Nicolson, her publishers. Though most eagerly awaited, it was a disappointment to some of her friends. Elizabeth is not an introspective person, being fascinated by every human being, with the single exception of herself. 'The main weakness in this self-portrait is that she does not seem to be particularly interested in herself,' commented the perceptive Philip Ziegler. Roy Jenkins was among those who felt some dissatisfaction with Elizabeth's benignity, writing that 'some hills might stand higher if the whole landscape were not painted quite so fair'.

By contrast, Elizabeth welcomed the task of compiling *Poets' Corner*, her penultimate book, published by Chapmans in 1992. This was an anthology of the poets and writers who have been commemorated in Poets' Corner in Westminster Abbey, along with a brief biographical note on each. The selection was left to her, enabling her to make a subjective choice based principally on childhood memories, personal taste and friendship – she had known seven of the poets she included: Gilbert Murray, John Masefield, T. S. Eliot, David Jones, Robert Graves, Edmund Blunden and Wystan Auden. She followed no chronological order, although the war poets are grouped together. The enthusiasm she brought to this task is infectious, and reflects the deep enjoyment that she has always gained from English literature and her broad knowledge of it.

III Royalist Writer

The Royal House of Windsor was a delightfully 'gossipy' text on George V, Edward VIII, George VI and Elizabeth II. Readers enjoyed the book, which contributed to Elizabeth's growing reputation as a royal commentator. *Louisa, Lady in Waiting* was published by Jonathan Cape in 1979. Louisa, Countess of Antrim, not herself a member of the royal family, was Lady in Waiting to Queen Victoria and Queen Alexandra, and as well as a diary kept numerous programmes, tickets, menus, itineraries, etc. From these Elizabeth created a delightful book in which her text connected and made sense of all Louisa's memorabilia.

The Queen Mother, published six years later, in 1981, was commissioned by Marks & Spencer, who were looking for a lightweight pictorial biography for their expansion into bookselling. It was not an easy undertaking because Elizabeth had no possibility of obtaining authentic sources such as letters or diaries, which are not available during the lifetime of members of the royal family. She therefore had to rely on her own knowledge. Before the book was completed, the store abandoned the idea of selling books, and *The Queen Mother* was finally published by Weidenfeld and Nicolson for the general market, where it was indifferently received. Several critics thought that the subject, with its patently unsatisfactory source material, was unworthy of Elizabeth's talents.

Elizabeth had hardly finished this work before she embarked on the more difficult project of a biography of Queen Elizabeth II. Again she had no authentic documents, for the Queen never gives interviews, but since the accession Elizabeth has attended many official occasions. She is also held in trust by the Queen and senior members of the royal family. Thus Princess Margaret agreed to meet Elizabeth, giving her considerable help on the early life of the Queen. The Princess saw Elizabeth twice and read the draft of the completed text, from which she eliminated some myths and to which she contributed additional details on the childhood years. It so happened that the 1982 party for Authors of the Year, given by the bookshop Hatchards, took place later on the same day as Elizabeth had lunched with Princess Margaret. Elizabeth and Antonia were among the guests, as was the Queen, who had a brief conversation with Antonia, telling her that she had heard that Elizabeth's lunch with her sister had gone well. The Queen's opinion is important to Elizabeth and she therefore noted with pleasure a story heard from two different sources: the Queen was engaged in a discussion on intelligence, at which the question came up, 'Why are clever women never nice?' 'They are sometimes,' said the Queen. 'Lady Longford is' (*Diary*, 28th July, 1983). In gathering material for *Elizabeth R*, Elizabeth received help also from former prime ministers, MPs, academics and courtiers.

Shortly before *Elizabeth R* was published in 1983, it was serialised in the *Daily Mail*. Financially the book was a great success. It enabled Elizabeth to assist with the private education of Paddy's sons – Paddy having retired from the Bar two years earlier.

Despite the problems that Elizabeth had encountered in acquiring source material, the critics were generally well disposed towards *Elizabeth R.* This biography, which took a year to research and another to write, changed some perceptions: the Queen was seen to be reticent rather than shy and her early childhood was not, as had been previously perceived, boring. The critic Kenneth Rose described the book as the most illuminating portrait yet to appear. More important to Elizabeth were the letters she received from the royal family: Prince Philip, Prince Charles and Princess Margaret all wrote in appreciation of the book.

In 1985 Elizabeth was approached by the Oxford University Press to compile an anthology of royal anecdotes. She did not hesitate; she would enjoy the research, much of which could be done in the London Library. The project was to take four years and culminated in an entertaining and popular volume, published in 1989 and issued as a paperback two years later. 'Ideally every anecdote should have a touch of something that is either "funny-ha-ha" or "funny-peculiar",' Elizabeth wrote in the introduction.[9] The anecdotes began in AD 61 with Boadicea and ended with Princess Diana's marriage to Prince Charles in 1981. Readers found the book both scholarly and amusing.

Two years later Weidenfeld and Nicolson published Elizabeth's *Darling Loosey*, the letters written to the artist Princess Louise, Queen Victoria's sixth child, by members of her family. The letters span the period 1856–1939 and are mostly in the royal archive at Windsor. Elizabeth was invited to edit the letters and introduce them with an essay on the Princess's life. The book afforded considerable pleasure, both to Elizabeth who was delighted to be working at Windsor again, and to her fascinated readers.

In 1992 Elizabeth was eighty-five and not long recovered

from the serious spinal operation she had undergone in 1989. It was a tribute to Elizabeth's credentials as a royalist and a serious writer that she was then commissioned by the publisher John Curtis to write a brief analytical book on the future of the monarchy, for publication in June 1993, the fortieth anniversary of the coronation. Elizabeth began by writing to a number of friends asking for comments on the monarchy and the changes that might be needed to allow it to survive. On the day after she had posted her letters, the Duke and Duchess of York announced their separation. Later it was disclosed that the Princess Royal was divorcing Captain Mark Phillips. In June, Andrew Morton's *Diana, Her True Story* was serialised in the *Sunday Times*, exposing the sham and unhappiness of what even then was still believed to have begun as a fairy-tale romance. It was over; the separation between the Prince and Princess of Wales was announced in November 1992.

Elizabeth's letters had not hinted at these troubles and she wondered whether anyone would take her seriously in the light of such ignorance. Moreover the straightforward book that she had planned became irrelevant when the Morton revelations were succeeded in December 1992 by the disclosure of the 'Camillagate' tapes. She had to make constant changes to the text; even when the book went to press early in 1993 there was still doubt about whether the *Sun* would pay damages for having leaked the Queen's Christmas message of 1992. (Eventually the newspaper apologised and paid £250,000 to a charity nominated by the Queen.) In addition to the problem of the continually developing stories, Elizabeth was under the pressure of time. She had agreed to write the book in nine months, but then John Curtis decided to advance the publication date by three months. Elizabeth accepted the revised timetable, but could only achieve it by postponing the family Christmas. She trusts no one else with her Christmas shopping, but that year they all had to wait for their Christmas presents until February when *Royal Throne* was finally concluded.

The difficulties of the subject were to an extent counter-balanced by royal confidence. Elizabeth received a welcome telephone call from Charles Anson, the Queen's Press Secretary, to say that the royal family was aware of Elizabeth's active support and would like to help her in any way possible. Sir Robert Fellowes, the Queen's Private Secretary, has remarked to the author that 'Elizabeth is one of the few commentators on the royal family who can really speak with authority because she has done the research, she is accurate and immensely conscientious . . . and she writes with an understanding of human nature . . .'

This willingness to help materialised in an interview with Prince Charles; the issues to be discussed were prearranged. Prince Charles sent a car to bring Elizabeth to Highgrove, where she taped an hour's interview. The tape was later returned to Windsor archive, where it awaits future historians.

In writing of the marriage of the Prince of Wales, Elizabeth was hampered by her own partisanship. Objectivity, that essential tool of the historian, sometimes eluded her. At times Elizabeth's editor, Linda Osband, had difficulty in persuading her to be fair to Princess Diana and to present a balanced overall view. Elizabeth holds horoscopes, tarot cards and what she regards as similar superstitions in such disdain that anyone relying on them forfeits her respect. Furthermore, she had a great deal more sympathy with Prince Charles, who had to cope with his wife's illness, than with Princess Diana, the patient. It may well be that years of coping with Paddy's illness had left Elizabeth with a greater understanding of the difficulties of the families of patients than of the patients themselves.

Difficulties notwithstanding, the book was approved by Prince Charles's office and published in April 1993, to a mixed reception. Roy Hattersley believed that the future of the monarchy was too trivial to occupy Elizabeth's talents. Ian McIntyre of *The Times* berated her for 'lifting' too much from *Hansard.* John Grigg of the *Spectator* lauded Elizabeth's balanced view, saying that 'her emergence as critic as well as apologist makes her all the more effective'. Unlike her major biographies *Royal Throne* must inevitably date and cease to be of interest; the book stands as testimony to Elizabeth's credo rather than to her literary achievement.

12

A Personal Perspective

'The stupendous event, the titanic endurance, the blaze of glory, the oceans of blood deflected him not an inch from his accustomed brevity and restraint.' So Elizabeth described the laconic style used by the Duke of Wellington to announce his victory at Waterloo.[1] Her own style is vivid, humorous, fast-moving. She makes use of copious information, conscientiously tracks down every source and is never overwhelmed by her findings. *Victoria RI* and the two-volume Wellington biography testify to an intellect shaped and disciplined in the Oxford tradition of Literae Humaniores. These works have justly earned the respect of academics and the approval of a large general readership: they will not easily be surpassed.

Judged by her first two biographies, the remaining body of Elizabeth's work is disappointing; their subject matter lacks the stature of an imperial ruler or the victor of Waterloo. *A Pilgrimage of Passion* is probably the best of her later books, but, although colourful, Wilfrid Scawen Blunt was never a major figure. Elizabeth's decision to concentrate on lesser works was deliberate. She was seventy-three in 1979 when *Pilgrimage of Passion* was published and by then she had made up her mind not to leave a half-finished manuscript for one of her children to complete.

Elizabeth has always said that biography 'found' her, and the same might be said of politics. In 1930, fresh from the 'unreality' of her golden Oxford years, she plunged into teaching students of the Workers Education Association in the Midlands. Shocked by the poverty and unemployment around her, and realising that political action alone could bring about the fundamental changes required, she moved swiftly from political indifference to radical support for the Labour Party.

For the next fourteen years, from 1930 to 1944, she was an active Labour Party supporter, but the promise detected by many was never quite fulfilled. At Cheltenham in the 1935 general election she did as well, if not better, than could have been expected of any Labour candidate. But in Birmingham she resigned before she could be put to the test of the electorate. An emerging radical in the early thirties, Elizabeth joined with communists to welcome hunger marchers to Cambridge, supported Stafford Cripps and his Socialist League and identified herself with all the activities of the local Labour Party in Cowley. Then, after her resignation in 1944 as a parliamentary candidate, her political fire seemed to falter, becoming little more than a flicker of support for Frank.

Elizabeth is known to have withdrawn from active political life because of the priority she affords to the needs of Frank and the children. That she has acted on this principle is not in doubt, nor can her loyalty to the Labour Party be questioned, for when some of its members broke away to form the Social Democratic Party, she was never tempted to join them. Yet in some areas her choices have been out of step with those of a radical socialist.

The two inheritances that came to Frank in 1938 affected Elizabeth minimally. She and Frank became the owners of considerable property but, aware of the contradiction between their principles and such ownership, the additional resources were soon expended on worthy and, as it happened, unsound schemes. On the other hand, Elizabeth's deliberate decision to opt for private education for all her children is considered by many to be a serious breach of socialist principle. This was a joint decision made by Elizabeth and Frank, both of whom retain their passionate belief in equal opportunity. The decision was not taken lightly but, having considered all the arguments, Elizabeth believed that it was her duty as a parent to provide the best available education for her children. In this case, therefore, her duty to her children had to take precedence over every other consideration. Nevertheless, she would like to see the present two-tier system of private and state schooling reformed.

Schooling is not the only issue on which Elizabeth has been faced by the dilemma of principle. When she required treatment for the tumour on her back in 1988, she sought it in a private hospital in south London, not under the NHS. Given Frank's position as Knight of the Garter and a senior politician with over twenty years' service on Labour's front bench, Elizabeth lives modestly. Many of her Oxford friends, such as Hugh Gaitskell, John Betjeman and Quintin Hogg, were to become figures of national importance, and when she married Frank she was drawn into his aristocratic circle. Hence, although Elizabeth's friends come from all walks of life, many are notable and privileged. When she came down from Oxford she moved with ease between wealth and poverty; she was equally at home with the Astors at Cliveden or the Hobsons in Stoke-on-Trent. On her own territory of Stairways and in all her subsequent houses she opted for a comfortable, modest and upper-middle-class style of life. Elizabeth's concern has always been with people; rank and wealth are of comparatively minor interest. Nevertheless, privileged life probably played a part in taming the radical flame that fired Elizabeth's early years.

Elizabeth has also moved away from her original republican sympathies. Having grown up in a nonconformist household, she regarded herself as outside the Establishment, perhaps even in opposition to it. Her marriage to Frank, involving her in Court functions, presentations and garden parties and the annual Garter ceremony, began to wear away her republican sympathies. Of greater importance, however, has been her preoccupation with Queen Victoria and her descendants. While researching *Victoria RI*, Elizabeth increasingly identified with her subject. 'I could understand the contrary pulls in Queen Victoria between her family and her public life . . . she had ten times more public life than I had and one more child – her nine to my eight – though she also had more help in the home' (*Pebbled Shore*, p. 308).

Elizabeth pursued her royal interest through her many books and in doing so has become an increasingly ardent monarchist. Her present position is very different from that of the young woman of 1935 who argued in Cheltenham that the House of Lords was rotten with decay. Sixty years on, in the 1990s, her support for Tony Blair and New Labour is as unequivocal and ardent as her support for the monarchy. This double allegiance would have been unthinkable in the days when she first joined the Labour Party. There are some who believe that, in making this shift to the right, Elizabeth has herself become an example of New Labour.

Similarly, Elizabeth's conversion to Roman Catholicism is sometimes interpreted as a mark of the Labour Party's emergence from a narrow sectarian past. When Frank became a Catholic in 1940, the Oxford Labour Party was so antithetical that they considered deselecting him as a prospective candidate. This is a situation that is hard to imagine in the 1990s, when Tony Blair often accompanies his Roman Catholic wife to mass.

As a high profile convert Elizabeth has also had some influence in the Roman Catholic Church. She has often been invited to write for the main Catholic papers and in 1993–4 was writing a regular column for *The Universe*. Common sense and pragmatism based on her experience of a successful marriage and a large united family have given her an influential voice with the laity, if not always with the hierarchy. She is herself a firm believer, goes regularly to mass and has no doubts about the afterlife; she is convinced that she will 'see' Catherine again, although how this will come about, she does not know. Loyal Catholic though she is, Elizabeth is not uncritical of the Church's teaching. She believes that women should be in charge of their own fertility, has come to accept her children's second marriages and is convinced that divorce is a more honest policy than annulment.

Elizabeth's wit and unflagging interest have ensured her popularity. She is one of those rare people who will spend an hour or more recounting all the literary and political gossip of the day without uttering one word that is unkind.

At this stage it is not possible to assess Elizabeth's influence on public affairs, but her influence on her own family is less ambiguous. She has been a powerful role model for her children and grandchildren; it can hardly be an accident that many have become successful writers. She has demonstrated to them the attractions of a career that provides protection from intrusion and release from domestic chores. It is surely no accident either that Elizabeth's daughters are no cooks!

More important, it is Elizabeth who has managed to keep her competitive, volatile and complicated family together in relative harmony. Bernhurst offers a focus, but Elizabeth is the magnet. Revelling in her role as a grandmother, which provides all the pleasures of children but few responsibilities, she sees herself as the repository for family news and a guarantor of continuity. With Bernhurst divided into 'Frontstairs' and 'Backstairs' she has achieved her ambition of simplifying the practicalities of life. There she can have the children and grandchildren around her, and space for her writing. She can continue to garden, which remains her favourite occupation. Were Frank not so involved with the House of Lords, Elizabeth would spend more time in Sussex, but life without Frank is unthinkable.

Some casual acquaintances receive the impression that Frank's need for Elizabeth is the greater; friends who know the Longfords well are aware that dependence is mutual. Frank is

Elizabeth's link with the 'real' world of politics, her main literary critic and adviser, her unfailing companion and source of amusement. In all their years of marriage they have never known a moment's boredom in each other's company; they have never been unfaithful and constantly exchange loving notes. Like every married couple, they had their problems in the early days, but Elizabeth does not accept that they had to work at their marriage. The most she will say is that it has become second nature to them to consider what the other may want. Each believes that the other's unselfishness is the key to the success of their marriage, a marriage that has come to be regarded as a national institution.

Appendices

Letter from Eliza

An extract from a letter to the author from Eliza Chisholm, a granddaughter of Elizabeth Longford.

I remember thinking 'Granny' a quite unknowable presence in the huge universe of relations. I suppose she was almost at the height of her writing life in the late sixties and early seventies, and had not yet fully 'grannified' herself.

It was not until Bernhurst became two houses [1978] with room for a whole family to stay and yet not invade, that we found a granny who liked talking to us. She remembered things we'd told her, kept track of our friends' names, took our opinions seriously. She wore red trouser suits and Indian jewellery, swam everyday with Grandpa in the green pool and managed always to look elegant and pretty. She said 'darling' in the warmest voice I'd ever heard.

She wanted to know the inside story on everything because she sensed that you wanted to tell it, not because she was ever nosey. I can't believe how dull it must sometimes have been, talking to an eleven year old about her pony, especially when she was never interested in horses herself. She always made you feel you had revealed something wonderful to her and that she was eternally grateful. She never smiled only with her mouth and not her eyes, like some adults did, so you knew she was really listening. And I think her lack of complaint/fuss about her growing deafness has shown everyone exactly how to behave when the same thing happens to us.

She was/is always working, but made it look easy, just like jotting down a couple of things before tea. Even though she was very busy and keeps about twenty things juggled in the air at once, she never makes you feel panic-stricken about wasting her precious time. In fact she does the opposite, she gives you the soothing impression that she has all the time in the world for you.

When I was a teenager Granny became more and more useful as a source of adult information. We specially liked hearing family history. She was very good at digging up stories about all the aunts and uncles as teenagers themselves. She was careful to say something complimentary about whatever we were wearing when we changed for dinner – though I expect it was often not to her taste at all. She never compared the various grandchildren in a way to make any of us feel inadequate.

Chronology

1906	Birth of Elizabeth Harman
1916	Pupil at Francis Holland School, Baker Street
1920	Pupil at Headington School, Oxford
1925	Gained scholarship to Lady Margaret Hall
1926	Undergraduate at Lady Margaret Hall
1927	Met Frank Pakenham
1930	Obtained degree
1931	Engaged to Frank Pakenham
1931	Married Frank Pakenham
	Moved to Stairways, Stone
1932	Birth of Antonia
1933	Birth of Thomas
1934	Moved to Singletree, Oxford
1935	Labour candidate for Cheltenham
1936	Adopted as Labour candidate for King's Norton
1937	Birth of Paddy
1938	Frank inherited Bernhurst and house off Park Lane
1939	Rented house in Birmingham
	Moved to Water Eaton Manor, near Oxford
1940	Frank became a Roman Catholic
	Moved to 8 Chadlington Road, Oxford
	Birth of Judith
1941	Suspension at King's Norton Labour Party
	Death of Roger Harman (brother)

1942	Birth of Rachel
1943	Birth of Michael
1944	Resigned from King's Norton
	Became a member of the Church of England
1945	Death of Nat Harman (father)
	Frank created Baron Pakenham of Cowley
1946	Birth of Catherine
	Received into Catholic Church
1947	Moved to 10 Linnell Drive, Hampstead
	Birth of Kevin
	Member of rent tribunal for Paddington & St Pancras
1950	Labour candidate for Oxford City in general election
	Moved to Bernhurst
1952	Acquired 14 Cheyne Gardens as London base
1953	Columnist for the *Daily Express*
1955	Publication of *Points for Parents*
1956	Silver wedding
1957	Birth of Rebecca Fraser, first grandchild
1959	Publication of *Catholic Approaches*
1960	Publication of *Jameson's Raid*
	Death of Katherine Harman (mother)
1961	Frank became seventh Earl of Longford on the death of his brother, Edward
1963	Move from Cheyne Gardens to Chesil Court
1964	*Victoria RI* published
1965	Guest at New Orleans 150th anniversary of battle
1968–78	Trustee of National Portrait Gallery
1969–75	Member of Advisory Council of the Victoria & Albert Museum
1969	Publication of *Wellington: The Years of the Sword*
	Death of Catherine
1972	Publication of *Wellington: Pillar of State*
	Received Honorary Doctorate of Letters, Sussex University

	Elected Fellow of the Royal Society of Literature
1974	Awarded C. B. E.
	Publication of *The Royal House of Windsor*
	Publication of *Churchill*
1975	Publication of *Byron's Greece*
1976	Publication of *Life of Byron*
1976–80	Member of the British Library Advisory Board
1979	Publication of *A Pilgrimage of Passion*
	Publication of *Louisa, Lady in Waiting*
	Appointed Honorary Life President of Society of Women Writers & Journalists
1980	Publication of *Images of Chelsea*
1981	Publication of *The Queen Mother*
	Publication of *Eminent Victorian Women*
	Golden wedding
1983	Publication of *Elizabeth R*
	Promotional tour of South Africa
1986	Publication of *The Pebbled Shore*
1987	Birth of Stella Powell Jones, first great-grandchild
1989	Spinal operation
	Publication of *The Oxford Book of Royal Anecdotes*
1991	Publication of *Darling Loosey*
	Diamond wedding
1992	Publication of *Poets' Corner*
1993	Publication of *Royal Throne*
	Portrait painted of Elizabeth and Frank by Lucy Willis
1996	Ninetieth birthday celebrations

Thomas Pakenham, = Elizabeth Cuffe,
cr. 1st Baron Longford 1756 | cr. Countess of Longford 1?

Edward, 2nd Baron,
m. Catherine Rowley

Georgina Beauchamp = Thomas, 2nd Earl, | Maj.–Gen. Ed. Michael GCB
cr. Baron Silchester | (1778–1815; died at
Battle of New Orleans)

Victor, 7th Earl of Jersey = Margaret Leigh | Edward, 3rd Earl | William, 4th Earl, | Francis = Caroline Ward
m. Selena Rice-Trevor | (Great Aunt Caro
(1842–1938)

8th Earl of Jersey, | Beatrice, | Arthur Child Villiers DSO | Mary Child Villiers = Thomas, 5th Earl | Edward
m. Cynthia Needham | m. Lord Dunsany | (1879–1933) | (1864–1915) | (Uncle Bingo
(Uncle Eddy)

Edward, 6th Earl | Margaret | Mary | Violet, | Julia, | Francis, 7th Earl = Elizabeth Ha
(1902–61) | (Pansy), | (Maria), | m. Anthony Powell | m. Robin Mount | (Frank) | (1906–)
m. Christine Trew | m. Henry Lamb | m. Meysey Clive | | | (1905–)

Hugh Fraser[1] = Antonia = [2]Harold Pinter | Thomas, | Paddy,
m. Valerie McNair Scott | m. Mary Plumr

Rebecca, | Flora, | Benjie, | Damian, | Orlando | Natasha | Maria | Ned | Fred | Eliza, | Richard | Guy,
m. Edward | m. [1]Robert | m. Lucy | m. Paloma | | | | | | m. Alex | | m. Kia
Fitzgerald | Powell Jones | Roper-Curzon | Porraz | | | | | | Chisholm | | Page
| [2]Peter Soros

by [1]

Blanche | Atalanta | Honor | Stella | Thomas | Eliza | William | Hugh | Ana Sofia | Aidan

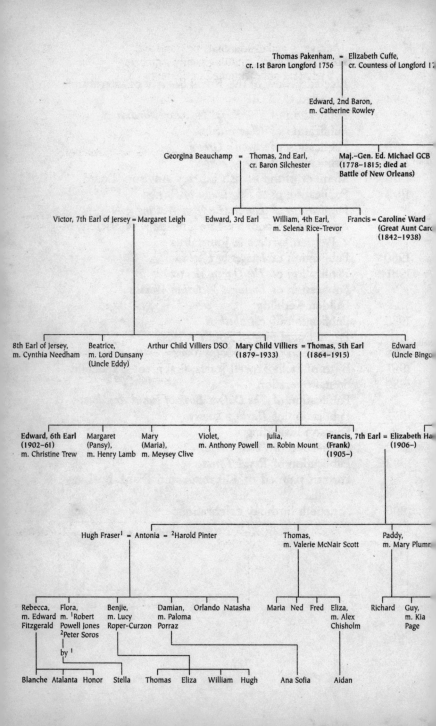

Ancestors and descendents of Frank and Elizabeth Longford, omitting family members who are not mentioned in the text

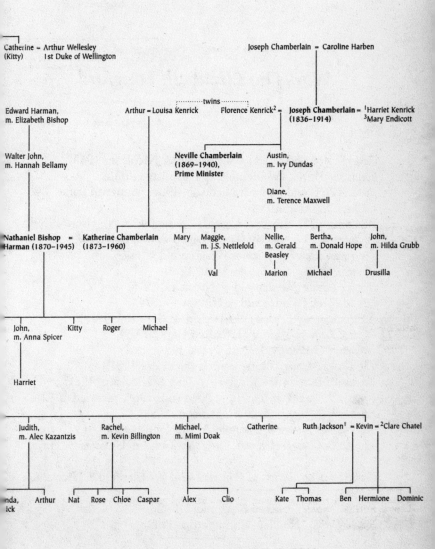

Catherine = Arthur Wellesley
(Kitty)   1st Duke of Wellington

Joseph Chamberlain = Caroline Harben

·········· twins ··········

Edward Harman,
m. Elizabeth Bishop

Arthur = Louisa Kenrick   Florence Kenrick² = Joseph Chamberlain = ¹Harriet Kenrick
                                                 (1836–1914)   ³Mary Endicott

Walter John,
m. Hannah Bellamy

Neville Chamberlain   Austin,
(1869–1940),   m. Ivy Dundas
Prime Minister

                       Diane,
                       m. Terence Maxwell

Nathaniel Bishop = Katherine Chamberlain   Mary   Maggie,   Nellie,   Bertha,   John,
Harman (1870–1945) (1873–1960)   m. J.S. Nettlefold   m. Gerald   m. Donald Hope   m. Hilda Grubb
                                                                         Beasley

                                                    Val   Marion   Michael   Drusilla

John,   Kitty   Roger   Michael
m. Anna Spicer

Harriet

Judith,   Rachel,   Michael,   Catherine   Ruth Jackson¹ = Kevin = ²Clare Chatel
m. Alec Kazantzis   m. Kevin Billington   m. Mimi Doak

nda,   Arthur   Nat   Rose   Chloe   Caspar   Alex   Clio   Kate   Thomas   Ben   Hermione   Dominic
ick

Works by Elizabeth Longford

Catholic Approaches (ed.) (Weidenfeld & Nicolson, 1953)
Points for Parents (Weidenfeld & Nicholson, 1956)
Victoria RI (Weidenfeld & Nicolson, 1964; winner of James Tait
    Black Memorial Prize)
Wellington: The Years of the Sword (Weidenfeld & Nicolson, 1969)
Wellington: Pillar of State (Weidenfeld & Nicolson, 1972)
The Royal House of Windsor (Weidenfeld & Nicolson, 1974)
Churchill (Sidgwick and Jackson, 1974)
Byron's Greece (Weidenfeld & Nicolson, 1975)
Life of Byron (Weidenfeld & Nicolson, 1976)
A Pilgrimage of Passion (Weidenfeld & Nicolson, 1979)
Louisa, Lady in Waiting (Jonathan Cape, 1979)
Images of Chelsea (St Helena Press, 1980)
The Queen Mother (Weidenfeld & Nicolson, 1981)
Eminent Victorian Women (Weidenfeld & Nicolson, 1981)
Jameson's Raid (Weidenfeld & Nicolson, 1960, reissued 1982)
Elizabeth R (Weidenfeld & Nicolson, 1983)
The Pebbled Shore (Weidenfeld & Nicolson, 1986)
The Oxford Book of Royal Anecdotes (Oxford University Press,
    1989)
Darling Loosey: Letters to Princess Louise (Weidenfeld & Nicolson,
    1991)
Poets' Corner (Geoffrey Chapman, 1992)
Royal Throne (Hodder & Stoughton, 1993)

Further Reading

Elizabeth Longford: *The Pebbled Shore* (Weidenfeld & Nicolson, 1986)

Mary Craig: *Longford: A Biographical Portrait* (Hodder & Stoughton, 1978)

Frank Longford: *Born to Believe* (Jonathan Cape, 1953)

Frank Longford: *Five Lives* (Hutchinson, 1964)

Frank Longford: *The Grain of Wheat* (Collins, 1974)

Frank Longford: *Avowed Intent* (Little, Brown & Company, 1994)

Violet Powell: *Five Out of Six* (Heinemann, 1960)

Violet Powell: *Within the Family Circle* (Heinemann, 1976)

Notes

1 Growing Up in a Puritanical Household

1 Katherine was always known as Katy, but for the sake of clarity
   her full name has been used throughout the book.
2 Joseph Chamberlain (1836–1914), mayor of Birmingham and
   national statesman, held various offices. His sons were also
   eminent. Sir Austen Chamberlain (1863–1937) became Chancellor of the Exchequer and Foreign Secretary, while Neville
   Chamberlain (1869–1940) was Chancellor of the Exchequer
   and, from 1937 to 1940, Prime Minister.
3 The Unitarians originated in Poland and Hungary in the
   sixteenth century. Their beliefs reached England in the following
   century. According to the *Oxford Dictionary of the Christian Church*,
   Unitarians follow 'a type of thought and practice which rejects
   the doctrines of the Trinity and the divinity of Christ in favour
   of the unipersonality of God'.
4 Elizabeth was called Betty until she was twenty, when she asked
   her family and friends to use her full name. To avoid confusion,
   the name Elizabeth has been used throughout the book.
5 Alison Debenham was the daughter of Cecily Kenrick, who had
   married Ernest Debenham, the founder of the department store
   Debenham & Freebody. Alison became an artist.
6 The school is referred to as Miss Nuth's in the Francis Holland
   School records, but as Miss Newth's in Elizabeth Longford's
   Pebbled Shore.
7 Founded by Charlotte Mason in 1887, PNEU is now known

as the Worldwide Educational Service and advises parents on the teaching of children aged between three and eleven at home.

8   The Zoological Society of London was founded in 1826. After 1940 the public were admitted to the zoo on Sunday afternoons, leaving Sunday mornings reserved for members and fellows.

9   Founded in 1897 by the then Bishop of Rochester, with the support of his friend Elizabeth Wordsworth, great-niece of the poet, the first Principal of Lady Margaret Hall, Elizabeth's future college. Years later Elizabeth was to make a radio appeal for the Settlement.

10 Dr Dawson, created Viscount in 1936, was physician to King George V and King George VI.

11 Gervase Mathew, OP (1905–76), lecturer in Patristics, was a member of several faculties of Oxford University, including History, Anthropology and English. A well-known spiritual director, he instructed several converts including Penelope Chetwode, the wife of John Betjeman.

2 Oxford at her Feet

1   Interview with Angela Levin in the *Sunday Times*, 1st February 1981.

2   John Betjeman: *My Oxford* (Robson, 1977).

3   Published by Jonathan Cape, 1953.

4   Philip M. Williams: *Hugh Gaitskell* (Jonathan Cape, 1979)

5   1907–; elder son of Douglas Hogg (1872–1950). A distinguished lawyer, Douglas held the office of Lord Chancellor in 1928–9 and 1935–8 and was created first Viscount Hailsham in 1929. Quintin was MP for Oxford City 1938–50. He left the House of Commons on inheriting his father's Viscountcy. He was First Lord of the Admiralty 1956–7. The Peerages Renunciation Act of 1963 enabled him to disclaim his peerage. Like his father, he became Lord Chancellor, 1970–74 and 1979–87. His son Douglas is, at the time of writing, Minister of Agriculture.

6   Author in conversation with Lord Hailsham.

7   Theodore Wade-Gery was Fellow and Tutor in Ancient History

at Wadham 1919–38, later Wykeham Professor of Ancient History at Oxford.

8   Naomi Mitchison, 1897–, was the daughter of the distinguished philosopher and philologist J. S. Haldane. She became a radical socialist and prolific writer. In 1916 she married Gilbert Richard Mitchison (1894–1970), eminent lawyer and Labour politician, created Lord Mitchison in 1964.

9   All students had to return to college by 11.15 p.m. In exceptional circumstances the Principal or Vice-Principal might grant an extension to midnight on the payment of a small fine.

10 Gaius and Tiberius Gracchus were both Tribunes of the People in Rome in the second century BC; they championed much-needed reforms and met violent deaths, Tiberius in 133 BC, Gaius in 121 BC.

11 Oxford finals are staggered throughout the summer term according to subject. Traditionally Greats examinations are the last to be held.

3 Approaching Marriage

1   A non-political, non-sectarian, non-vocational organisation founded in 1907 to bring the finest university education to those whose formal schooling had ended at twelve or earlier.

2   Founded 1911 by Major the Hon. Arthur Child Villiers, Frank's uncle, to provide a sports facility for poor children in Hackney. It is now an educational trust, giving Sixth-Form courses and based at Villiers Park, Middleton Stoney near Bicester.

3   1906–48; gained a first in Modern Greats at Oxford in 1927, lectured also at New College, Oxford; member of War Cabinet Secretariat, elected MP 1945, Parliamentary Private Secretary to Hugh Dalton, Chancellor of the Exchequer; writer on economic affairs.

4   In 1961, on the death of Edward, the sixth Earl of Longford, Frank became seventh Earl. The castle and lands, however, were inherited by Thomas Pakenham, Frank's eldest son and the present owner. He restored the castle's original name, Tullynally.

Elizabeth Longford

5   Frank was thrown twice during the course of one race. He remounted both times, but, concussed and disoriented after his second fall, he set off in the wrong direction, narrowly avoiding a head-on collision.

6   The Hadow consultative committee was originally set up in 1899 under the Board of Education Act. It was reconstituted under Sir William Hadow (1859–1937) in 1920 and issued three reports: *The Education of the Adolescent* (published 1926); *Primary Education* (1931); and *Infant and Nursery Schools* (1933). This advocated secondary education for all, rather than for a privileged 10 per cent, and two types of secondary school: grammar and secondary.

7   Violet Powell: *Within the Family Circle* (Heinemann, 1976), p. 105.

8   Canon Carnegie's first wife, Albinia Crawley, died in 1902. In 1916 he married an American, Mary Endicott, the third wife of Joe Chamberlain.

4 Settling in to Married Life

1   Violet Powell: *Within the Family Circle* (Heinemann, 1976), p. 180.

2   Esmond Warner was the son of the cricketer 'Plum' Warner and the father of the writer Marina Warner.

3   Debutantes were presented at Court when they left school and entered society and were then presented a second time after their marriage. All presentations had to be made by a sponsor, who must have been presented herself and who was therefore acceptable to the Lord Chamberlain who was responsible for the Court. Between the Second World War and 1958, when presentation parties ceased, the presentations became limited to debutante girls; married women merely looked on.

4   Her first marriage was to the Earl of Jersey, after whose death she married Ronnie Slessor.

5   Dr Chadburn (1868–1957) promoted the advancement of women in medicine. She founded the South London Hospital for Women and was largely responsible for the foundation of the Marie Curie Hospital in 1928.

6   Sir Stafford Cripps (1889–1952), President of the Board of Trade

1945, Chancellor of the Exchequer 1947, was known for his policy of austerity imposed by tough controls and the continuation of rationing.

5 A Full Life

1   'Ernie' Bevin (1880–1951) became a leader of the trade union movement, merging more than twelve trade unions to form the TGWU in 1922. Unusually for a socialist, he opposed pacifism in the 1930s, urging rearmament. In 1940 he entered Parliament and from 1940 to 1945 was Minister of Labour and National Service. From 1945 to 1951 he served as Secretary of State for Foreign Affairs.

2   Beatrice Potter married Sidney Webb in 1892 and they made a significant contribution to the improvement of social and industrial conditions of their day, serving on many commissions. They were prominent in the Fabian Society.

3   Adolf Hitler and his extreme right-wing National Socialist (Nazi) party had achieved power constitutionally in Germany in 1933. Hitler destroyed Germany's democracy and withdrew the country from the League of Nations and from the Disarmament Conference, which the League had fostered. In defiance of the Versailles Peace Settlement of 1919, drawn up by the victors of the First World War, Hitler began to rearm Germany. In March 1936, in a further breach of the Versailles Treaty, he reoccupied the Rhineland and two years later forced Austria into union with Germany. Next he demanded the Sudetenland from Czechoslovakia which the Czechs, bowing to pressure from France and Britain, agreed to cede, but in March 1939 German troops then marched into Prague and what was left of Czechoslovakia was destroyed. Neville Chamberlain, Prime Minister of Britain from 1937 to 1940, had acted on the belief that Hitler could be contained by a policy of appeasement, but after the Munich Agreement was broken by the invasion of Czechoslovakia, the British government gave guarantees to Poland and attempted to gain support from Soviet Russia, an attempt that was pre-empted by the Nazi-Soviet Non-Aggression

Pact of August 1939. When Germany invaded Poland, war was inevitable.

4 Neville Chamberlain, Prime Minister from 1937 to 1940, believed that Hitler could be contained by a policy of appeasement, but after the Munich Agreement was broken by the invasion of Czechoslovakia, the British government gave guarantees to Poland. When Germany invaded Poland, war was inevitable.

5 There is some confusion about the timetable of events. Several members of the family insist that Frank kept his conversion from Elizabeth for six years; Frank and Elizabeth maintain that it was hardly six hours.

6 Problems of War

1 Letter to the author.

2 William Beveridge (1879–1963) was a social reformer and architect of the welfare state. He was created a Baron in 1946.

3 Founded in 1884 with the aim of establishing a democratic socialist state by evolution rather than revolution. Its members included George Bernard Shaw, Sidney Webb and Annie Besant.

7 Changing Directions

1 *Humanisme Intégral* by Jacques Maritain (1882–1973), published Paris; English translation by M. R. Adamson.

2 Frank Longford, seventh Earl, 1905–. Created Baron Pakenham of Cowley 1945. Knight of the Garter 1971. Lord in Waiting 1945–6, Parliamentary Under-Secretary for War 1946–7, Chancellor of the Duchy of Lancaster 1947–8, Minister of Civil Aviation 1948–51, First Lord of the Admiralty May–October 1951, Chairman of National Bank 1955–62, Lord Privy Seal 1964–5, Secretary of State for Colonies 1965–6, Lord Privy Seal 1966–8, Chairman of National Youth Employment Council

1968–71, Chairman of Sidgwick & Jackson 1970–80.
3   Harriet Harman, who was elected Labour MP in 1982 and has served in the Shadow Cabinet since 1992, was the third of their four daughters.
4   The Borgia popes Callistus II (Alfons de Borgia), 1455–8, and his nephew Alexander VI (Rodrigo de Borgia), 1492–1503, led scandalous lives and brought condemnation on the Church.

8 A Political Family

1   Hugh Gaitskell had been appointed Under-Secretary to Emmanuel Shinwell, the Minister of Fuel, in 1946.
2   Conversation with the author.
3   From Peter Stanford's biography of Lord Longford (Heinemann, 1994, p. 207.
4   Conversation with the author.
5   The First Lord of the Admiralty, as political master of the Royal Navy, held Cabinet rank until 1964, when his responsibilities passed to the Secretary of State for Defence.
6   No attendance allowances or expenses were paid to peers until 1957. In 1951 only those peers who had government appointments received a salary.

9 Impending Tragedy

1   William Maxwell Aitken (1879–1964), created Baron Beaverbrook in 1917, was of Canadian origin and sought to exercise political influence in Britain through acquiring newspapers. He acquired the *Daily Express* in 1916 and launched the *Sunday Express* in 1918 and the *Evening Standard* in 1923.
2   Fr Paton, CSC (1909–92), opened his campaign in the USA in 1946 by means of radio broadcasts. This was the first of many visits in which he attempted to persuade families to sign a pledge to say a daily rosary together.
3   Sir Hugh Fraser (1918–84) served in the Lovat Scouts, the family

regiment and the SAS in the Second World War. Elected Conservative MP for Stone, Staffordshire, 1945. Held ministerial office 1958–62.

4   In July 1956 Britain and the USA withdrew support for the Aswan High Dam in Egypt, which Colonel Nasser, Egypt's dictator, was building. A few days later Nasser nationalised the Suez Canal. Attempts at negotiations foundered and on 1st November France and Britain under the leadership of the Prime Minister, Sir Anthony Eden, and in collusion with Israel, launched an air and sea attack against Egypt. On 5th and 6th November British and French troops landed at Port Said and advanced south, but pressure from the Americans forced the British to withdraw. The episode was universally condemned and it effectively ended Eden's political career.

5   See *Women on Women*, ed. Margaret Laing (Sidgwick & Jackson, 1971), p. 227.

6   'As I See it', *The Universe*, 3rd October 1993.

7   'As I See it', *The Universe*, 28th August 1994.

8   The Peerages Renunciation Act of 1963 enabled hereditary peers to renounce titles for their lifetime. It did not allow for the renunciation by the first holder of a peerage; therefore Frank's acceptance in 1945 of the barony of Pakenham continued to exclude him from the House of Commons.

9   Frederick Edwin 'F. E.' Smith (1872–1930), a barrister, entered Parliament in 1906. Created Baron Birkenhead in 1919, he held office as Lord Chancellor from 1919 to 1922 and was created the first Earl of Birkenhead in 1922. He became friendly with Frank Pakenham in his final years. His son, Frederick, the second earl, (1907–75) was Frank's best man and married Sheila Berry, daughter of the first Viscount Camrose. Sheila's brother, William Berry, married Pamela Smith, the second earl's sister, in 1936.

10 Conversation with the author.

11 The Château of Hougoumont was one of the key strongpoints on the battlefield. It was attacked by the French, who forced the main gate. With great courage the defending guards closed the gates, killed all the invading force except one drummerboy and, according to Wellington, saved the day, and thus ultimately won the Battle of Waterloo.

10 'Early Afternoon'

1   By Rosalie Shann, 24th September 1972.
2   In 1965 Ian Brady and Myra Hindley were sentenced to life imprisonment for the murder of Lesley Anne Downey, aged ten, John Kilbride, aged twelve, and Edward Evans, seventeen. Brady and Hindley made tape recordings and took photos of their victims; this shocked and revolted the public.
3   Interview with Jean Rook, 1972.
4   Conversation with the author.
5   Letter to the author.
6   In 1947, by the Wellington Museum Act, the house and contents were transferred to the nation by the seventh Duke. By the terms of the Act, the house was to be used partly as a museum and partly as a residence. The Wellington Museum was opened to the public in 1952.
7   The storm was said to have been the worst since that of 1703, although the human cost was in no way comparable. About 8000 people lost their lives in 1703, against seventeen in 1987. On the other hand, damage to property was severe; gardens and woodlands were devastated.
8   Letter to the author from David Uttley, FRCS.

11 Author of Distinction

1   The library was opened in 1960. The papers of Neville and Austen were later added to those of their father, Joseph, in the Chamberlain Room of the Special Collection Suite.
2   Black dyes were not always fast, and were considered a health hazard at the time.
3   Sir Henry Ponsonby (1825–95) was Queen Victoria's Private Secretary from 1870 to 1895. His papers contain the letters that he wrote from Court to his wife. Charles Greville (1794–1865) was a well-known diarist and gossip.
4   *Victoria RI*, p. 265.
5   *Victoria RI*, p. 160.
6   Conversation with the author.

7   *The Guardian*, interview by Catherine Stott, 1969.
8   Elizabeth knew of this *via* her friend Malcolm Muggeridge's book on the Missionaries of Charity, *Something Beautiful for God* (Collins, 1971).
9   *The Oxford Book of Royal Anecdotes* (Oxford University Press, 1989).

12 A Personal Perspective

1   *Wellington: The Years of the Sword*, p. 569.

Index

Index

Dudley, Lord 113–14
Dufferin and Ava, Basil, Lord 56
Dufferin and Ava, Maureen, Lady 56
Dunsany, Beatrice, Lady 50
Dunsany, Eddie, Lord 50, 52, 61, 122–3
Durbin, Evan 33, 35, 47, 52, 98–9, 100, 113, 114
Düsseldorf 111

Eden, Sir Anthony 128
Edinburgh, HRH Prince Philip, Duke of 112, 123, 172
Edmund Campion (Waugh) 106
Edward VIII, see Windsor, Duke of
Elcho, Lady 167
Eliot, George 169
Eliot, T. S. 170
Elizabeth II, HM Queen 112, 122, 123, 150, 160, 171–2, 173
Elwes, Simon 110
Eton Manor Boys' Club 34
Erasmus 30
Essex Unitarian church, Notting Hill 9

Family Ties 109
Favell, Fr 90, 96, 103
Fawcett, Bice 87, 107
Fellowes, Sir Robert 174
Fenton (N. Staffs) 38
Fitzwilliam Museum, Cambridge 165
Forsyte Saga (Galsworthy) 42
Foyle, Christina 135–6
Francis Holland C of E School for Girls 13
Fraser, Antonia (née Pakenham) 49, 54, 56, 57, 63, 66, 73–4, 75, 79, 81, 82, 83, 84–5, 87, 89, 90, 96, 98, 101, 105, 107–8, 109, 110, 111–12, 117–18, 119, 124, 125, 127, 137–8, 143–4, 149, 153, 167, 171
Fraser, Flora 131, 151
Fraser, Hugh 127, 137, 143, 144
Fraser, Rebecca 129
Fritillary 30

Gaitskell, Arthur 26, 27–8
Gaitskell, Dora 119
Gaitskell, Hugh 22, 24, 25, 26, 27, 28, 30, 52, 98, 108, 113, 116, 119, 131–2, 178
Galsworthy, John 42
Gardner, Helen 133, 134
Garvin, J. L. 156
Gascoigne, Bamber 168
Gate Theatre, Dublin 40, 67

General Strike (1926) 30
Geoffrey Chapman (publishers) 170
George V, HM King 54
George VI, HM King 112
Girl Guide Association 18
Gladstone, W. E. 161
Glendalough 56
Godolphin School (Salisbury) 105, 108
Goldsmith, Harry d'Avigdor 29, 132
Goldsmith, Sarah d'Avigdor 132
Gollancz, Victor 111
Gordon Walker, Patrick 98, 107
Graham, Alastair 36
Graves, Robert 170
Greenwood, Anthony 63
Greenwood, Arthur 63, 99
Grenoble University 18–19
Greville, Charles 159
Greycote's School (Oxford) 108
Grier, Linda 31
Grigg, John 174–5
Grinter, Ellen 145
Grocott, Leah 34, 35
Grove, Valerie 138

Hadow Report (1926) 42
Hailsham, Douglas, 1st Viscount 28
Hailsham, Quintin, 2nd Viscount 28, 98, 116, 128, 178
Hales, E. Y. 157
Harman, Anna 100–1
Harman, Elizabeth, see Longford, Elizabeth
Harman, Harriet, 198
Harman, John 3, 5, 6, 7, 8, 9, 10, 11, 12, 15, 100–1, 152–3
Harman, Katherine 1–2, 3, 4, 5, 6, 7, 8, 10, 12–13, 14, 15, 16, 19, 20, 23, 27–8, 30–1, 47–8, 53, 56, 61, 65, 68, 87, 88, 96–7, 101, 116, 131, 152, 156
Harman, Kitty 3, 4, 5, 6, 9, 11, 14, 15, 47, 56, 168
Harman, Michael 3, 5, 10, 11
Harman, Nathaniel (Nat) 1, 2–3, 4, 5, 10, 11, 12–13, 14, 16, 18, 20, 23, 39, 46, 55, 68, 87, 88, 96–7, 101–2, 126, 146
Harman, Roger 3, 5, 11, 88, 89, 95, 97
Harman, Walter 2, 3
Harrod, Roy 61
Hartley, L. P. 45
Hatfield House 52, 71
Hattersley, Roy 174

207